The Lead

The Follower

To lead with greatness, one must first learn to follow with grace.

1st Edition

Michael W. Compton

Table of Content

Introduction Section..1

Chapter 1: Followership 9

Chapter 2: The EmpowerTrust Dynamic...24

Chapter 3: Direct Empathetic Communication.........................42

Chapter 4: Having Fun 62

Chapter 5: Self-Care as Leaders and Followers.........................78

Chapter 6: Combating Burnout 101

Chapter 7: Caring Not to Care 117

Chapter 8: The Harmony of Spheres – Mastering Work-Life Balance..127

Chapter 9: Changing Hands...147

Chapter 10: Bridging the Generational Gap...............................170

Chapter 11: The Difficult Talk (Followership).............................186

Chapter 12: The Difficult Talk (Leadership) 207

Chapter 13: Leading Up: The Following Leader 220

Chapter 14: Listen Up and Read 235

Chapter 15: The Brillant Non-Manager......................................250

Chapter 16: The Road Ahead...261

The book, The Leader The Follower, and the brand Like Minded Leadership are copyright trademarks.

Copyright © 2024 by Michael Compton

All rights reserved. No part of this book or brand may be reproduced, distributed, or transmitted in any form or by any means, including photocopying, recording, or other electronic or mechanical methods, without the prior written permission of the publisher, except in the case of brief quotations embodied in critical reviews and certain other noncommercial uses permitted by copyright law. For permission requests, email the publisher, addressed "Attention: Permissions Coordinator," at the email address below.

Contactus@weareleadership.com

ISBN: 9798329822779

Library of Congress Control Number: 2024913411

This is a work of nonfiction. The experiences and perspectives shared in this book are based on the author's personal journey and are intended to inspire and provide insights into leadership and followership. Any references to historical events, real people, or real places are used fictitiously. Other names, characters, places, and events are products of the author's imagination, and any resemblance to actual events or places or persons, living or dead, is entirely coincidental.

Printed in the United States of America

First Edition: July, 2024

Compton, Michael
The Leader The Follower / Michael Compton.
ISBN 9798329822779

Disclaimer: The information provided in this book is for educational and informational purposes only. The author and publisher make no representations or warranties with respect to the accuracy or completeness of the contents of this book and specifically disclaim any implied warranties of merchantability or fitness for a particular purpose. The advice and strategies contained herein may not be suitable for your situation. You should consult with a professional where appropriate. Neither the author nor the publisher shall be liable for any loss of profit or any other commercial damages, including but not limited to special, incidental, consequential, or other damages.

This book is dedicated to my son William. *"May you always follow your heart and lead with unwavering passion. Love always, Dad."*

Introduction

I'm grateful you chose to delve into this book. In an era of endless information and available content, it's truly an honor to be a part of your journey.

Although this book is about leadership, it transcends conventional concepts and dives into followership. It's also a small window into my transformation, sculpted by extraordinary individuals and pivotal moments. Allow me to introduce myself: My name is Mike Compton. Over the past 15 years, I've journeyed from a call center representative to Vice President of Technology.

You might wonder how a Vice President of Technology came to write a book on leadership, followership, and individual development. The answer lies in the rich tapestry of experiences and lessons I've gathered. My journey has been far from linear, filled with both formidable challenges and remarkable opportunities. Each step taught me invaluable lessons about what it truly means to lead and, just as importantly, to follow.

When I first thought of composing a leadership book, the task seemed daunting, and a bit of a mad idea. I am not a professional writer, and my primary school English grades were less than thrilling. However, as my favorite actor, the late Robin Williams, once said, "You are only given one small spark of madness; you mustn't waste it." And I didn't.

I drafted this book to share my journey, thoughts, and feelings on leadership and followership, hoping to provide a sense that you are never alone in the battles we often face in leading people and being led by others. My hope is that you take from this book what you value and mold it into your professional life, empowering you to move forward, regardless of where your path has taken you.

When I was five years into my career, I encountered some amazing influential figures, and my life took a turn. These encounters were serendipitous, sparking changes in ways I couldn't have anticipated. When I accepted a seemingly ordinary management position at a local credit union, I was motivated by financial gain and the prestige of a higher managerial title. I was oblivious to the profound personal growth awaiting me. This foundational experience taught me the importance of empathy, effective communication, and the ability to stay calm under pressure—skills that became the bedrock of my leadership philosophy.

Over the years, I have opened my eyes, mind, and heart to the wonders of change, learned behaviors, and the magic of leadership.

As I advanced into managerial and then executive roles, I encountered new hurdles that tested my resilience and adaptability. From navigating organizational changes to spearheading innovative projects, each experience offered profound insights into the nuances of leadership. Throughout this journey, I was fortunate to be mentored by some truly extraordinary individuals. Their wisdom and guidance were instrumental in shaping my approach to leadership. They taught me that true leadership is not about wielding power but about empowering others, developing a collaborative spirit, and maintaining a clear vision even in the face of adversity.

These experiences led me to read my first authentic leadership book, "Developing the Leader Within You" by John Maxwell, a transformative read that reshaped my approach. This book, alongside the wisdom of other leadership luminaries, compelled me to reflect and evaluate the person I was, both in my professional and personal life.

At 23, I learned the pivotal lesson of genuinely listening to my colleagues, team, and, most importantly, my wife. I realized I wasn't the center of the universe, the smartest, or always right. Humility and self-reflection were not inherent to my younger, more headstrong self, who believed his knowledge was divine.

My mentors guided me toward self-reflection and self-forgiveness, nurturing an inner dialogue that emphasized thoughtfulness over impulsivity. This transformation was about curbing my "gift of gab" and adopting a genuine engagement with the world around me—a lesson of listening more than speaking.

The most profound lesson was learning to follow before leading. As the best lessons often are, this experience was hard-earned. In the early stages of my career, I was driven by a naive ambition for rapid advancement. Fresh out of college and full of enthusiasm, I believed that climbing the corporate ladder quickly was the hallmark of success. I eagerly took on new roles and responsibilities, often biting off more than I could chew.

One particularly humbling experience came when I was promoted to a team lead position. I was excited to prove myself, but my inexperience and overconfidence soon led to mistakes. I remember one instance where I mishandled a critical project deadline, causing delays and frustration among my team. My initial reaction was to blame external factors, but deep down, I knew I had overcommitted without understanding the intricacies of effective teamwork and project management.

It was during this challenging period that I began to understand the foundational value of followership. I realized that to lead effectively, I first needed to practice better followership. This meant listening more than speaking, observing more than directing, and appreciating the expertise and contributions of my colleagues.

This realization was a turning point. I started to focus on internal learning, seeking feedback from peers and subordinates alike. I took the time to understand the dynamics of my team, learning from their experiences and expertise. I embraced humility, recognizing that my growth as a leader depended on my ability to follow and learn from others.

This period of introspection and growth was not without its setbacks. There were moments of self-doubt and frustration, but each challenge reinforced the importance of patience and perseverance. Gradually, I began to see the positive impact of this shift in approach. My relationships with my team improved, and we started to achieve our goals more effectively.

Looking back, those early struggles and the lessons learned were invaluable. They taught me that effective leadership is not about rapid advancement or personal accolades, but about establishing a collaborative and supportive environment. It's about having the humility to follow before you can truly lead.

As my journey has continued along a path of limitless possibility, I have sought opportunities to share the lessons I learned with others. Now that I look beyond my own reflections, I am passionate about followership and leadership, and how to bring those concepts to others. My mentors' guidance was a spark that ignited my desire to elevate their ideas, teachings, and values. Now, I am forging forward to offer my unique philosophy of authentic leadership and followership.

Before you begin reading the rest of this book, reflect for a moment on the mentors who played a pivotal role in shaping your identity. What lessons have they revealed, and how have those teachings influenced your approach to leadership, followership, collaboration, and personal growth?

Many seek guidance from mentors, books, or influential figures who they hope will illuminate their path. In this book, I propose an alternative perspective: the mentor's role is not to dictate your journey but rather to inspire you to engage in self-reflection so you can carve out a path that is uniquely yours.

This book embodies that philosophy. My writing does not provide exact answers but provokes thought, challenges your ideals, and encourages a deeper exploration of your convictions and aspirations. Consider this book a catalyst to ignite your personal growth, exploring the lessons and insights I have gathered along my own journey. Each chapter is designed to delve into specific aspects of these roles, offering practical advice, personal anecdotes, and strategies for success.

For more information on my Like-Minded Leadership initiative, to contact/connect with me, and for general information please visit my website – www.weareleadership.com Or use the QR code for my website:

Please feel free to follow and connect with me on LinkedIn:
https://www.linkedin.com/in/mikecomptonleadme/

Use the QR code below for my LinkedIn profile:

I also produce a regular newsletter via my LinkedIn page. Use the QR code below to access my newsletter:

Consider listening to my podcast – Leading the Way by Mike Compton (Available on Spotify, Amazon Music, Apple, and iHeart)

Use the QR code below to access my podcast on Amazon:

Here's a brief overview of what you can expect:

Chapter 1: Followership
We begin with the foundation of leadership: which is followership. This chapter explores the crucial role of being a good follower and how it shapes effective leaders. We'll look at real-life examples and discuss the importance of humility, learning, and support within a team dynamic.

Chapter 2: The EmpowerTrust Dynamic *(Copywriter Michael Compton, All Rights Reserved)*
Building on the basics of followership, we dive into the EmpowerTrust Dynamic, a concept central to developing strong, trust-based relationships within teams. Learn how empowering your team members and establishing trust can transform your leadership approach.

Chapter 3: Direct Empathetic Communication *(Copywriter Michael Compton, All Rights Reserved)*
Effective communication is the cornerstone of leadership. This chapter focuses on the art of direct yet empathetic communication, providing techniques to convey your message clearly while maintaining empathy and understanding.

Chapter 4: Having Fun
Leadership doesn't have to be all serious business. Discover how incorporating fun and enjoyment into your leadership style can boost morale, enhance creativity, and strengthen team bonds.

Chapter 5: Self-Care as Leaders and Followers
Self-care is essential for both leaders and followers. This chapter highlights strategies for maintaining physical, mental, and emotional well-being, ensuring you can perform at your best.

Chapter 6: Combating Burnout – A Path to Sustainable Success
Burnout is a common challenge in high-stress environments. Learn practical steps to identify, prevent, and combat burnout, paving the way for sustainable success for yourself and your team.

Chapter 7: Caring Not to Care
Balancing empathy and objectivity is a delicate act. This chapter

discusses how to care effectively without becoming overwhelmed, maintaining a healthy balance between emotional involvement and professional detachment.

Chapter 8: The Harmony of Spheres – Mastering Work-Life Balance
Achieving work-life balance is crucial for long-term success and happiness. Explore strategies for harmonizing your professional and personal spheres, ensuring a fulfilling and balanced life.

Chapter 9: Changing Hands
Transitions in leadership can be challenging. This chapter offers insights on how to navigate these transitions smoothly, whether you're stepping into a new role or passing the baton to a successor.

Chapter 10: Bridging the Generational Gap
In today's diverse workforce, understanding and bridging the generational gap is essential. Learn techniques to foster collaboration and mutual respect among team members of different ages.

Chapter 11: The Difficult Talk (Followership)
Confronting challenges and addressing issues is part of followership. This chapter provides guidance on how to have difficult conversations as a follower, offering constructive feedback and addressing concerns effectively.

Chapter 12: The Difficult Talk (Leadership)
Similarly, leaders must also engage in tough discussions. Learn how to approach these conversations with confidence and empathy, ensuring they lead to positive outcomes.

Chapter 13: Leading Up: The Following Leader
Leadership isn't just about directing those below you; it's also about influencing those above. This chapter explores the concept of leading up, offering strategies for effectively managing your relationship with higher-ups.

Chapter 14: Listen Up and Read
Active listening and continuous learning are vital for growth. Discover how to enhance your listening skills and cultivate a habit of lifelong learning to stay ahead in your leadership journey.

Chapter 15: The Brilliant Non-Manager
Not all leaders hold managerial titles. This chapter celebrates the brilliance of non-managers who lead by influence, offering insights on how to harness and nurture this often-overlooked leadership style.

Chapter 16: The Road Ahead
In the final chapter, we look to the future. Reflect on the journey we've taken together and explore the ongoing path of leadership and followership, equipped with the tools and insights to navigate whatever comes next.

Chapter 1: Followership

The Essence of Followership

Followership begins with a fundamental truth often shadowed by the allure of leadership: without influential followers, leadership is devoid of purpose and impact. Followership is active engagement in supporting and executing a leader's or an organization's vision. It's a dynamic role characterized not by passivity but by active listening, critical thinking, constructive feedback, and a commitment to the team's success.

John Maxwell once said, "A leader without followers is just a person taking a walk." This is one of my favorite sayings. And over the years, as I've reflected on this quote, I've realized that to become a leader with followers, I must first understand the needs of my potential followers. I need to know what would inspire them to follow me. Recognizing the importance of committing to followership myself. By demonstrating my dedication and belief in others, I could earn their trust and belief in me as their leader.

Followership is more than just offering support; it's about actively contributing to the goals and vision of a leader or organization. It involves shaping the vision rather than simply following it. Effective followership, characterized by qualities such as reliability, initiative, collaboration, and commitment to common objectives, is a powerful force. It also promotes independent critical thinking and constructive feedback, giving each follower a voice and influence in the organizational dynamics. Followership is the understanding that to be a great leader, one must first be a great follower.

Being a follower means having the ability to trust and care for another person, wanting them to succeed, and being their pillar of support and motivation. Adopting followership means expanding the definition of being a follower into the essence of being a leader. This concept is not limited to your direct manager; it applies to anyone you can support. Whether it's your boss working towards a large objective, your peer working on a project, or your followers tackling a difficult task, followership is essential.

Both leadership and followership are dynamic. As a leader, there will be times when you need to be direct, decisive, and drive progress. However, there are also times when it's essential for you as a leader to shift into a follower role, offering unwavering support to others. Whether you are the CEO driving the strategy of your organization, someone starting out in your career aiming for lofty advancements, or an independent contributor moving large objectives forward, the mechanics of followership can be applied and adopted to help you succeed. By doing so, you can gain the respect and trust of your organization and set the tone and expectations. A great organization, team, family, or any group is not built on a single individual leading the way forward. It is built on many individuals playing the part of leader and follower, using their unique gifts to achieve unified objectives. Natural leaders must invoke followership to allow non-natural leaders the ability to shine and move their organization forward.

Unfortunately, our societal emphasis on leadership sometimes obscures the equally, if not more, important role of followership.

Take interviews for example. If you are interviewing for a new job, how often do you hear the question, "Describe your leadership style"? Has anyone ever asked you, "Describe your followership style?" Try it next time and see what answers you receive. Although I'm typically quick on my feet, I would not have been prepared to answer this question in my earliest job interviews.

Instead, I can hear my inner 20-year-old reassuring myself, "I am a leader. Strong, reliable, honorable." That is what I hoped I was.

When I introduced the question of followership style in interviews, the varied, often uncertain responses highlighted a widespread oversight: the unpreparedness to articulate one's role as a follower. Witnessing people struggle to describe followership underscores the need for a cultural shift—recognizing a follower's critical role in any organization's success. Instead of focusing solely on leadership qualities, we must prepare to be influential followers, ready to adapt, learn, and contribute toward our shared goals.

For me, it all started when I was transitioning from my first corporate career organization to another. I was interviewing and fully prepared to talk about how great of a leader I was. "I did this, I did that." While it's important to "sell yourself" in an interview, I now realize I would have been more successful had I highlighted more supportive examples of my skills. Instead of focusing solely on my individual accomplishments, I wish I had emphasized how I supported others within my organization to be successful. This approach would have shown my potential new organization and leadership team that I was both an exceptional leader, capable and strong in driving progress, and an exceptional follower, agile and supportive of others who, in the moment, were in the spotlight. As I started to realize this, I also began to further notice those I was interviewing.

Most interviewees were prepared to talk about their leadership style, how they would execute, and what they had to offer. Not one of them took the time to think about how they would fit in as a follower in a new organization. They were focused on what they believed I wanted to hear, strong leadership skills, and dynamic answers.

When I started asking the specific question on followership in interviews, it became overwhelmingly clear that individuals were not prepared to answer. I received many different types of responses, ranging from "I am not a follower; I am a leader" to questions about taking the ring of power to Mordor (followership is not to be confused with fellowship), and everything in between. However, very few responses came close to understanding and acknowledging how followership is a cornerstone methodology in being an effective leader of people.

Now, if someone asked me how I would describe my followership style, here's what I'd say: "As a new employee or leader, my immediate role is not to come in and make changes. I must earn the respect of my team, coworkers, and leadership by showing that I can be as great a follower as I can a leader."

Expanding further, I would go into detail on how my decision-making abilities are minimal, as I observe. This allows me to follow others, preparing me to lead them more effectively someday. Developing followership skills is a crucial step in this journey. When we focus on being good followers, we learn to understand the needs and perspectives of those we aim to lead. This understanding becomes a foundation upon which strong, empathetic leadership is built.

In most settings, apart from the armed forces, positional-level leadership alone rarely works. Simply being the boss isn't enough to inspire genuine commitment and enthusiasm from your team. Yes, your employees may do what you say, but achieving true leadership requires more than issuing commands. Obedience might produce baseline results, but it is respect and loyalty that drive exceptional performance and innovation. The difference lies in how leaders engage with their team, creating an environment of mutual respect and trust. Following your team is just as important as leading your team. You have hired these individuals, or others have hired these individuals for their expertise and abilities. Let them work and follow their lead.

I would also work into the interview answer my leadership abilities that derive from the followership answer. Discussing the distinction between a boss and a leader: the boss is obeyed, while the leader is respected. A boss relies on authority to get things done, often focusing on immediate tasks and short-term goals. In contrast, a leader earns the respect and loyalty of their team by demonstrating integrity, showing appreciation for their contributions, and investing in their development. And by following their direct reports' lead. This respect and loyalty translate into a more committed and motivated team, willing to go above and beyond to achieve shared objectives.

Understanding and practicing followership is essential for anyone aspiring to be an effective leader. By mastering the art of followership, individuals can learn to navigate the dynamics of leadership, build stronger relationships, and ultimately create a more cohesive and high-performing team. And to become a great leader, one must first understand and excel as a follower. Mastery in any field, including leadership, is rarely instantaneous. Just as we wouldn't trust a surgeon who hasn't undergone rigorous training, we can't expect to become influential leaders without first learning to be effective followers.

The Traits of Effective Followership

Followership is not a passive or secondary role. Instead, it's an active and dynamic process involving listening, observing, learning, and contributing constructively to the group or leaders' goals. Good followers are not merely subordinates but collaborators who offer feedback, constructively challenge ideas, and bring unique perspectives.

Some might argue that emphasizing followership encourages passivity or unthinking obedience, undermining innovation and initiative. However, this misunderstanding conflates passive compliance with authentic followership's strategic and active participation. Effective followership is not subordination without thought; it's about choosing when to lead and when to offer support, recognizing that both roles are crucial to a team's success. This balance creates an environment where ideas are challenged constructively, and diverse perspectives and insights inform leadership.

Some traits of effective followership include:

1. Truly listening
2. Staying silent when appropriate
3. Allowing for small amounts of failure for the greater good of lessons learned
4. Balancing leading and following
5. Understanding a leader's vision
6. Adaptability
7. Responsibility/Accountability
8. Supportiveness
9. Providing constructive feedback

Followership involves understanding and aligning with the leader's vision. A follower must comprehend the leader's goals and objectives and work collaboratively to achieve them. Alignment does not imply visionless compliance; it requires critical thinking and a willingness to voice concerns or suggest improvements when necessary and appropriate.

Another critical aspect of followership is adaptability. A follower must be able to adapt to different leadership styles and environments. Each leader has their unique approach, and being an effective follower involves adjusting to these differences. This adaptability enhances a follower's ability to work efficiently under various leaders and in diverse teams.

Adaptability is not one-sided, either. A great leader will adapt to their followers' needs and feedback. This reciprocal adaptation is crucial for developing a harmonious foundation for a working relationship. A successful leader must adapt their approach to accommodate a diverse range of personalities, skill levels, experiences, and other unique factors in their team. When you practice adaptability as a follower, you are laying the groundwork for becoming a more versatile, responsive leader.

For instance, a leader might need to alter their communication style to ensure understanding among team members with varying experience levels or backgrounds. Similarly, a leader may need to modify their leadership style to better align with the strengths and weaknesses of individual team members to cultivate a more inclusive and productive environment.

Adaptability is crucial for navigating modern workplaces' dynamic nature. This type of adaptability might involve adjusting strategies to meet evolving business goals, reshaping team structures to optimize performance, or even reevaluating one's leadership philosophies in light of new challenges, organizational growth, and opportunities.

In addition to adaptability, followership is fundamentally about taking responsibility. Good followers don't just execute tasks; they assume ownership. Followers recognize that their actions significantly impact the team's success and take this responsibility seriously.

In my own experience, I have had to learn and relearn this lesson a few times. When working on projects, because I am what people consider a natural leader, I tend to take command very easily, overshadowing those I should be following. In doing so, I lose their respect and risk stifling what they can bring to the table, creating tension, and ultimately dividing the team we are attempting to lead toward success.

Learning to be adaptable, I have tried to work one-on-one with individuals. I strive to be open and transparent when I find myself slipping into the leadership role due to my overdeveloped natural leadership abilities. I meet with them, even for just 15 minutes, to acknowledge when I might have overstepped. I make it clear that they are the leaders and emphasize how important their role is to me as a follower on the project. This approach breaks down barriers and demonstrates my seriousness in respecting their leadership position. By applying followership in these types of situations, you can gain significant leadership points with that individual as well as others on the project team. In the future, the individual you have followed will likely follow you as their leader on the next project, or in general as a leader of your organization.

You never know how loyalty is born, but humility is key to capturing it. I often hear phrases like, "Heavy is the head that wears the crown," or, my favorite, "That's why you get paid the big bucks." These sentiments reflect a common practice of shifting all responsibility onto the leader—a mindset we can no longer afford. We must embrace equal responsibility, working as followers and leaders toward a common goal. Influential leaders already bear the weight of their actions and decisions, whether for better or worse. A follower who offers support, rather than merely noting their non-leadership role, sets everyone up for success.

Consider this scenario: You've just experienced a significant setback and approach your leader to inform them. By saying, "Well, you need to act since that's why you make the big bucks," you effectively wash your hands of the issue, implying, "Good luck with that; it's not my problem." Now, imagine a different approach: "This is a tough situation. What can I do to help us figure out the next steps? Be a sounding board? Take something off your plate?" This supportive stance exemplifies authentic followership.

Diving in deeper we can look at some of these examples.

1. Setbacks can come in many different forms. They might include the failure of a project, the loss of key employees, difficult audit findings, or any other unexpected challenges that add complexity and surprise. Each setback presents unique obstacles and requires a thoughtful approach to navigate and overcome.
2. For instance, the failure of a project can be disheartening, but it also provides an opportunity to analyze what went wrong, learn from the mistakes, and apply those lessons to future endeavors. The loss of key employees can disrupt workflows and morale, but it can also open the door to fresh talent and perspectives, prompting a reevaluation of team dynamics and processes.
3. Difficult audit findings might initially seem like a major roadblock, but they can serve as a crucial wake-up call, highlighting areas that need improvement and ensuring that the organization is operating with greater transparency and efficiency. Any unexpected challenge, regardless of its nature, forces us to adapt, innovate, and strengthen our problem-solving skills.

Ultimately, setbacks, while challenging, are an inevitable part of any journey. They test our resilience, creativity, and determination. By approaching them with a proactive and open mindset, we can transform these obstacles into valuable growth opportunities, paving the way for greater success in the future. By applying followership principles, overcoming these challenges will seem less like a steep upward solo climb and more like a manageable, hand-over-hand ascent. Where you are sometimes the leader, extending a hand to a follower, and more often a follower extending a hand to a leader.

A common pitfall among many leaders is the belief that they must always be at the forefront. Leaders feel compelled to generate the best idea, complete tasks first, and have all the answers. However, when you're in a followership role, it's crucial to attune to the room's dynamics and understand your leader's perspective. There are times when having the answer is necessary, but part of evolving into an effective leader involves learning to listen, pause, and let others take the spotlight. Being the best, fastest, and most original does not always guarantee advancement.

Early in my career as a leader, I believed that being the best leader meant being the first to speak and assuming that my ideas were always the best. I focused on giving commands and ensuring they were executed. However, I soon realized that while there are times to assert leadership and push forward with your ideas, effective leadership often involves creating opportunities for my team and peers to openly discuss their ideas. This approach leads to richer dialogue and greater overall buy-in, regardless of the direction that is chosen.

And while we understand that effective leadership is crucial, disastrous should you get it wrong; so, too, is effective followership. Poor followership can manifest as a lack of engagement, unwillingness to provide honest feedback, or failure to support the team's objectives. A team member who consistently withholds constructive criticism may hinder the team's growth, while one who follows without question may contribute to a culture of mediocrity. Recognizing these pitfalls is the first step toward avoiding them, fostering a culture where active, engaged followership is valued as much as leadership.

I used to believe that I needed to be constantly at the top of my game, leading and excelling in everything. This mindset was exhausting and ultimately counterproductive. However, things started to fall into place when I began to view myself as both a leader and a follower. This self-initiated, challenging journey of reflection is a process I am still actively working on. However, embracing the ongoing study and commitment to my philosophy of followership has significantly aided me in navigating the complex realm of leadership.

Followership in Practice: You Have Time to Build Your Skills, Take It!

Awareness and open discussions are the bread and butter of outstanding leadership and followership relations. As we have said many times already, cultivating qualities of effective followership lays the groundwork for becoming a great leader. The skills and insights gained from understanding how to be a follower of leaders—such as empathy, teamwork, critical thinking, and understanding diverse perspectives—are invaluable in shaping a well-rounded and effective leader.

You possess a unique ability to empathize with those you lead because you have walked in their shoes and likely continue to navigate your own journey of following a leader. This relationship can manifest at various hierarchical levels, such as an employee to manager, a manager to a director, and so forth. Each of these layers contributes to a complex and distinctive dynamic within the organizational structure.

Transitioning from an independent contributor to a managerial role too rapidly can impede your opportunity to deeply understand the nuances of followership. Without this crucial understanding, you might miss the chance to fully appreciate the perspectives and challenges faced by those you now lead. Recognizing and valuing the experience of being a follower is essential in developing the empathy and insight needed to be an effective and compassionate leader. This awareness helps to cultivate a more cohesive and supportive team environment, developing mutual respect and a shared sense of purpose.

Taking your time in each role you occupy is vital for several reasons. Firstly, it allows you to master the skills and responsibilities associated with that position. By fully immersing yourself in your current role, you gain a comprehensive understanding of the tasks, challenges, and intricacies involved. This deep knowledge not only makes you more competent but also builds credibility among your peers and subordinates. Secondly, spending adequate time in your current role enables you to develop strong relationships with your colleagues. These relationships are built on trust, mutual respect, and shared experiences. As you work alongside your peers, you learn to appreciate their strengths and understand their weaknesses, creating a foundation for effective collaboration when you eventually step into a leadership role. Thirdly, taking your time allows you to observe and learn from the leaders above you. Watching how they handle various situations, manage their teams, and make decisions provides invaluable lessons that can shape your own leadership style. You can adopt best practices, avoid common pitfalls, and refine your approach based on real-world observations.

Moreover, a gradual transition through roles provides you with the opportunity to experience different perspectives within the organization. This well-rounded view helps you develop a holistic understanding of the company's operations, culture, and goals. When you finally move into a managerial position, you do so with a wealth of knowledge and experience that enables you to lead with confidence and foresight.

The importance of taking your time in each role cannot be overstated. It lays the groundwork for effective leadership by ensuring you have the necessary skills, relationships, and understanding to succeed. By embracing the journey of followership and progression, you prepare yourself to become a leader who is not only skilled but also empathetic, insightful, and deeply connected to the team you will guide.

Too often, I see young and enthusiastic professionals attempting to leap from independent contributor to manager, then to director, and eventually to senior leader far too quickly. This rapid progression, or quantum leaping, should be approached with caution. While the desire to move up in an organization is certainly commendable, advancing too quickly carries certain risks. Trust me, you have time—plenty of it.

Embrace and enjoy your role as an independent contributor. As you ascend to higher positions where leadership becomes more prominent, take the time to master your craft in those leadership roles before looking for the next leadership level. It's essential to develop your leadership skills thoughtfully and gradually. By doing so, you can maintain a deep understanding and appreciation of the importance of followership to fully develop your leadership abilities.

Critical thinking is another essential aspect of developing personal awareness through followership. While leaders often focus on the larger picture, set expectations, and drive progress, independent contributors must critically analyze both simple and complex situations. They act on their conclusions, seek support, direction, and buy-in from their peers and leaders. Developing the ability to draw sound conclusions and effectively present them to leadership is deeply tied to critical thinking skills. Recognizing and valuing followership is vital for personal growth and building a culture where leadership and followership are seen as complementary and equally significant roles in achieving collective success.

Advancing too rapidly from an independent contributor to a leader can negatively impact the development of your critical thinking skills. A leader without well-honed critical thinking abilities may struggle to effectively teach and guide their team of direct and indirect followers. Critical thinking is essential for problem-solving, decision-making, and fostering an environment of growth and innovation. Without it, a leader may find it challenging to provide the necessary support and direction that their team needs to succeed.

Consider the example of Ernest Shackleton's Antarctic expedition, known as the Imperial Trans-Antarctic Expedition, which took place from 1914 to 1917. Shackleton's ship, the Endurance, became trapped in pack ice in the Weddell Sea and was eventually crushed and sunk. The crew endured extreme conditions, camping on the ice and later making a harrowing journey to Elephant Island. Shackleton and a small team then undertook an incredible open-boat voyage to South Georgia Island to seek rescue, ultimately saving all 28 crew members. Shackleton's leadership is rightly celebrated, but the mission's success also hinged on the crew's exceptional followership. The crew's ability to adapt, support each other, and stay committed to the mission under dire circumstances highlights the power of collaborative effort rooted in trust and mutual respect. Similarly, modern organizations thrive when employees at all levels engage in active followership, contributing to a shared responsibility and achievement culture.

Ernest Shackleton's career prior to the Imperial Trans-Antarctic Expedition exemplifies how experiences in non-leadership roles are crucial in developing exceptional leaders. As a young merchant navy officer and later as a third officer on Robert Falcon Scott's Discovery Expedition, Shackleton honed his skills in navigation, discipline, and teamwork. These formative years taught him the importance of empathy, resilience, and critical thinking—qualities that are indispensable for any leader. His time as a follower, particularly in the harsh conditions of Antarctic exploration, gave him a profound understanding of the challenges faced by his team members, enabling him to lead with compassion and insight.

Shackleton's leadership during the Nimrod Expedition and his preparation for the Imperial Trans-Antarctic Expedition were deeply informed by his earlier experiences. The technical knowledge, problem-solving abilities, and collaborative spirit he developed as a follower allowed him to make strategic decisions, maintain morale, and foster a sense of camaraderie among his crew. Shackleton's story highlights the invaluable lessons that come from taking the time to master each role, emphasizing that the journey of followership is essential in shaping a leader who is not only skilled but also empathetic and insightful. His career is a powerful reminder that leadership success is built on the foundation of understanding and valuing the follower's experience.

Personal Transformation at the Home Front

The profound impact of embracing followership in my personal life, extending beyond professional development, necessitated a pivotal shift. After mentors reflected on my workplace behaviors and attitudes, I recognized the need for introspection, which led to a significant transformation: I became calmer, learning to listen more and speak less. I realized I was not the sole navigator of my life's journey.

Understanding that my career achievements didn't automatically make me the de facto leader at home, I also started to appreciate the balance between leadership and followership within my family dynamics. I began stepping back sometimes, allowing my partner to lead while I offered support.

Too often, dynamic and natural leaders rise quickly through the ranks of their careers, sometimes creating a pay gap between partners. This dynamic often results in one person being automatically perceived as the leader and the other as the follower. As a young adult, I shared this opinion of home life positional power. I believed that if I made all the money, I would naturally be the leader. I couldn't have been more wrong. It took time to break this behavior trait, and occasional self-reflection is still needed, but learning to balance leadership and followership at home has served me very well. Adopting follower and leader roles in my personal life has been incredibly rewarding. It created a more equitable and respectful relationship where both voices are heard and valued. Moreover, it allowed me to exemplify these behaviors to my children, teaching them the importance of collaboration, mutual respect, and valuing diverse perspectives in family decision-making.

The behaviors we learn in childhood play a crucial role. Whether it's valuing personal happiness, recognizing that hard work leads to expected outcomes, or understanding the importance of work-life balance, these principles are essential for a fulfilling life. Personal happiness involves prioritizing what truly brings joy and satisfaction, while the belief that hard work equates to achieving desired results instills perseverance and dedication. Meanwhile, maintaining a healthy work-life balance ensures that neither professional nor personal well-being is neglected, helping to create the ability to develop self-inflicted overall harmony and contentment. These values together create a foundation for a well-rounded and meaningful existence. Which is all what we truly want for our children, isn't it? That is until they can start taking care of dear old dad, for which that will then be the sole focus of their day-to-day life. Right!?

As a parental figure, it's my responsibility to teach the importance of leadership, respect, sharing, manners, and knowing when to follow. Our children need to follow our lead, but it's equally important to sometimes follow theirs. Nurturing children who become influential adults is not a one-way street. Becoming a parent humbled me, and I have learned to follow my tenacious toddler to support a well-rounded individual. That is, until it's Lego time—when Dad morphs into a master builder, and our living room turns into a chaotic construction zone of epic proportions.

Embracing followership at home has harmonized my personal and professional relationships and enhanced my leadership across all areas of my life. As we navigate the complexities of professional and personal relationships, embracing the dual roles of leader and follower allows us to build more resilient, supportive, and effective teams. Valuing followership as much as leadership means we can develop an environment of mutual respect, learning, and growth. In this balanced ecosystem, individuals and organizations can flourish, paving the way for collective achievements that reflect the strength of our collaborative efforts.

Chapter 2: The EmpowerTrust Dynamic: The Art of Stepping Back for Empowerment

As you embark on your journey into people leadership, mastering the art of followership by stepping back and empowering those you lead will be crucial. A common pitfall in corporate America, particularly among those in management or higher positions, is inadvertently hindering productivity through excessive involvement. This over-involvement often arises from leaders attempting to be both the visionary/executor, and the finite detailed doers and decision makers.

And it all starts from the top down. When senior leaders micromanage, it creates a cascade effect, pushing lower-level managers to adopt the same approach. This dynamic can lead to a situation where managers become glorified department seniors, stifled by their leaders and, in turn, stifling their direct reports in an attempt to maintain a sense of productivity.

The detrimental effects of this leadership style are widespread. First, it undermines the autonomy of team members, stifling their creativity and initiative. When employees feel their every move is being scrutinized, or they are unable to make decisions or complete tasks within their job scope without their leader's buy-in, they are less likely to take risks or propose innovative solutions. This environment breeds a culture of dependency rather than one of proactive problem-solving and independent thought.

Second, over-involvement can lead to burnout for both leaders and their teams. Leaders who try to control every aspect of their team's work can quickly become overwhelmed, spreading themselves too thin and neglecting their strategic responsibilities. Meanwhile, team members may feel demoralized and undervalued, leading to decreased job satisfaction and higher turnover rates.

My followership's methodology of the EmpowerTrust Dynamic is to learn to lead by following your team. This is critical in combatting the challenges of over-involvement as a leader, hindering your own leadership abilities in the process. Leaders must embrace the principles of effective followership. This involves recognizing that stepping back and allowing team members to take ownership of their work can lead to greater overall success. By creating a culture of trust and delegation, leaders can empower their teams to operate more autonomously and efficiently. In this chapter, we will unpack how to counteract these tendencies.

Examining Leadership Overreach

One of the most significant challenges is finding the right balance between guiding your team and stepping back to let them thrive independently. This section delves into the common pitfalls that leaders face when they struggle to empower their teams effectively. We will explore the root causes and behaviors that contribute to diminished empowerment, such as inadequate team composition and the prevention of talent growth. By understanding these underlying issues and their impacts, you will gain valuable insights into developing a more autonomous and productive team environment.

>**Inadequate Team Composition**: If you frequently find yourself thinking, "It's easier to do it myself," this is a strong signal that you might not have the right people in the right roles. This could stem from challenging hiring practices or environment, a lack of understanding of each team member's strengths and weaknesses, or insufficient training and development. When team members are not well-suited to their positions, leaders may feel compelled to step in and take over tasks, leading to a cycle of dependency and reduced team autonomy.
>
>   a. **Behavioral Indicators**: Constantly redoing or correcting team members' work, reluctance to delegate important tasks, and a pervasive sense

of frustration or impatience with the team's performance.
   b. **Solutions**: Reevaluate your team's composition and identify any skill gaps or mismatches. Difficult conversations, which we will talk about later, will be critical in setting expectations, maintaining accountability, and generally being able to set your follower up for success.
      i. Invest in targeted and meaningful training programs to enhance the team's capabilities.
      ii. Implement a more rigorous hiring process to ensure that new hires are the right fit for their roles. Discuss with your leadership team that hiring the right person, rather than a body in a chair is important. Meaning the position may be open for longer than ideal, and the tasks left incomplete until the role is filled.
   c. **Root Causes**: The root of this issue often lies in poor initial team setup. Leaders might not have clearly defined the roles and responsibilities during the hiring process, or they may not have invested enough time in understanding the unique strengths each team member brings to the table. This lack of clarity can lead to mismatched expectations and underperformance.
   d. **Long-Term Impact**: Over time, this can lead to decreased morale as team members may feel they are not being utilized to their full potential. The persistent intervention of leaders can also lead to a lack of ownership and accountability within the team, further diminishing productivity and innovation.

Preventing Talent Growth: Over-involvement can signify that you're not allowing competent individuals to excel without interference. This behavior stifles the professional growth of team members by not giving them the space to take on challenges, make decisions, and learn from their experiences. When leaders do not trust their team to handle responsibilities, it impedes the development of leadership skills within the team, ultimately weakening the organization's overall leadership pipeline.

1. **Behavioral Indicators**: Micromanaging tasks, providing overly detailed instructions, rarely seeking or valuing team input on decisions, and a tendency to take credit for team successes while blaming others for failures.

2. **Solutions**: Practice conscious delegation by assigning meaningful tasks that challenge your team members and allow them to grow. Encourage a culture of open communication where feedback is valued and used constructively. Recognize and celebrate individual achievements to build confidence and motivation.

3. **Root Causes**: This often originates from a leader's fear of losing control or an ingrained belief that their way is the only way to achieve success. It can also stem from a lack of trust in the team's abilities, which might be due to past experiences or an inadequate onboarding process that didn't set the team up for success.

4. **Long-Term Impact**: Over time, talented individuals may become disengaged and look for opportunities elsewhere, leading to high turnover rates. This behavior can create a toxic work

environment where team members are afraid to take the initiative or make mistakes, stifling creativity and innovation.

Often, the reality is a combination of both, leading to a situation where top talent feels stifled due to a lack of accountability or clarity from leadership. Leaders who take over from underperformers without addressing the problem wind up with accountability issues. A leader who's trying to do too much can create an environment with a lack of clarity—bouncing from item to item or project to project can leave the rest of the team bewildered.

How often do you lie awake at night when a forgotten task comes barreling into your mind? Do you reach for your phone to send yourself a reminder email? Does that reminder email get lost in the several emails that came in before the following day?

As leaders, our ultimate goal is to inspire and enable our teams to perform at their highest potential. By understanding the nuances of managing leaders, avoiding process over-involvement, and steering clear of excessive oversight, you can cultivate a more empowered, engaged, and productive team environment. Let's examine these pitfalls and learn how to navigate them to enhance your leadership approach:

1. **Leaders Managing Leaders**: When senior leaders micromanage, resolving team issues, or excessively directing activity, it disrupts the organizational hierarchy. Over-involvement can make the manager seem more like an operational senior than the leader they are meant to be. However, this doesn't imply that you can't have a relationship with your manager's team; it's crucial to maintain the chain of command to ensure empowerment and engagement aren't diminished.

2. **Process Over-Involvement**: Leaders should refrain from taking over independent contributors' tasks. Doing so erodes team autonomy and hinders professional development. If you find yourself constantly being the "go-to" person, why do you have a team? Continually being the "go-to" points to a more significant issue, which your senior leadership team should address. Feeling over-involved in day-to-day activities could indicate a need to reassess staffing, manage rapid growth, or evaluate whether you have the right people on your team.

3. **The Pitfall of Excessive Oversight**: Flooding teams with non-essential questions or interrupting their workflow can significantly disrupt efficiency and morale. A leader who poses high-level, redundant, or off-the-cuff questions in larger meetings causes considerable disruption. While these questions may be necessary, they are better addressed in one-on-one discussions with your direct reports or smaller management-level meetings.

All the above, in some way, shape, or form, are signs that you, as the leader, need to step back and allow others to blossom as independent contributors. By addressing these underlying issues through strategic team composition and fostering an environment of trust and empowerment, leaders can break free from the cycle of over-involvement. This shift not only enhances individual and team performance but also builds a resilient and capable leadership pipeline for the future.

Practing the EmpowerTrust Dynamic philosophy can help combat many of these challenges.

Cultivating a Culture of Empowerment and Accountability

Effective leadership goes beyond overseeing tasks; it involves developing an environment where teams can excel independently while maintaining trust and accountability. Encouraging self-sufficiency, providing clear role definitions, and establishing a culture of trust are foundational elements in this approach. Leaders must balance guidance with autonomy to prevent overreach and stifling innovation. By nurturing talent and creating a clear framework for roles and responsibilities, leaders can focus on strategic foresight and long-term planning, ensuring that their teams operate efficiently in the present while navigating future challenges. This section delves into some of the EmpowerTrust Dynamic principles of encouraging independence, clear role definitions, and trust, offering practical insights into building a sustainable and empowered team.

1. **Adopt Independence**: Encourage self-sufficiency in your team. Provide guidance but resist the urge to intervene in every aspect of their work. If you sense their unease, provide motivational support, and avoid saying, "Let me just do it." Allowing your team to find their solutions advances confidence and innovation.

2. **Create Clear Role Definitions**: Ensure everyone understands their responsibilities and the extent of their decision-making powers. Job descriptions can be rigid, so having discussions to clarify roles and duties is essential. These discussions might need to happen multiple times throughout the year, especially in industries experiencing rapid growth or change. This responsibility falls on both managers and team members. As a leader, ensure clarity, and as a non-manager have the courage to speak up when job responsibilities are unclear.

    > **Industry Example**: In fast-paced sectors like finance and technology, regular discussions on duties, decision-making, and responsibility are crucial due to the constantly changing landscape. The FinTech space, in particular, requires continual adaptation and role clarification to keep up with its dynamic nature.

3. **Trust and Accountability**: Develop a culture where trust is paramount, and accountability is clear and well-defined. When your best and brightest see that accountability measures are in place and consistently applied, their trust in leadership grows. Transparency in holding individuals accountable creates a sense of fairness and reliability within the team. This is achieved by engaging in difficult discussions, practicing transparency, and often being direct to the point of making underperforming individuals feel uncomfortable enough to change their behaviors. This discomfort can lead them to accept guidance and coaching or, if necessary, move out of the organization. This doesn't mean you don't have to take this measure without empathy, which we will explore further in the next chapter.

A leader's role isn't just about ensuring immediate tasks are completed; it's fundamentally about cultivating an environment where the team can excel independently. Creating the conditions for excellence involves setting attainable goals, hiring and nurturing talent, and continually investing in their development. Leaders must trust their team to take the initiative. In doing so, they can shift their focus to longer-term strategies and visionary planning, much like anticipating several moves ahead in chess. Operating on a reactive, move-by-move basis can lead to missed opportunities and strategic setbacks. Effective leadership, therefore, is about creating a sustainable framework where the team operates efficiently in the present while the leader focuses on navigating the future.

Senior Leadership and Avoiding Becoming Obstacles

Senior leaders must avoid becoming the very roadblocks they're meant to remove. Although their roles often involve strategic planning, cultural development, policy review, audit undertakings, and boosting engagement, they sometimes need to engage in ongoing projects directly. This involvement, however, should be limited to short sprints for overcoming specific challenges.

Consider a scenario where a critical software implementation project is overdue, over budget, and mismanaged. Despite multiple rounds of leadership intervention and guidance, the project continues to falter. The development team is demoralized, deadlines are consistently missed, and the project's objectives seem increasingly out of reach.

In such cases, it is not feasible for a leader to remain on the sidelines. Direct involvement becomes necessary. The senior leader decides to step in, conduct a thorough project review, and hold a series of candid one-on-one discussions with the project leader and key team members.

During these discussions, the leader openly addresses the performance issues, asking pointed questions to understand the root causes of the delays and budget overruns. The conversations are uncomfortable, highlighting specific instances of mismanagement and underperformance. The leader sets clear expectations and outlines the consequences if improvements are not seen promptly.

For example, the project leader, who has been struggling to coordinate the team's efforts effectively, is given a choice: accept a comprehensive coaching plan designed to enhance their project management skills or transition out of the role. The leader also introduces stricter milestones and regular check-ins to monitor progress closely.

This direct approach, though uncomfortable, leads to significant changes. The project leader opts to undergo coaching, improving their ability to delegate tasks and manage the team more efficiently. Team members, witnessing the transparent handling of accountability, start to align better with the project's goals and timelines. As a result, the project begins to regain its footing, moving closer to completion within the revised budget and schedule.

This extremely high-level example, and while much easier to write out than to practice. Demonstrates that by creating an environment of direct communication, accountability, and support, leaders can turn around struggling projects and drive meaningful change, ensuring that individuals either step up to meet the required standards or make way for those who will.

At this juncture, you might wonder: if stepping in to rescue a project creates obstacles, what's the right approach? The key lies in subsequent steps. Did you implement the necessary accountability measures? Were tough decisions made and challenging conversations held? It's crucial to inform the team appropriately about the accountability and corrective actions.

Where we fail as leaders and drive high performers crazy is when we make excuses and allow continuing underperforming individuals to remain without consequences. By doing so, we become obstacles to our organization's progress, hindering its ability to move forward. High performers become frustrated and demoralized when they see their efforts undermined by a lack of accountability for those who consistently fail to meet expectations.

Yes, addressing performance issues publicly is difficult, but it can be done tastefully and constructively. When handled correctly, it sends a powerful message to the entire organization that accountability is a core value. This doesn't mean humiliating individuals or airing all details of their shortcomings. Instead, it involves transparent communication about the importance of meeting standards, the steps being taken to address performance issues, and the support being provided to help individuals improve.

For instance, during team meetings, leaders can discuss the importance of accountability and share general examples of how performance issues are being managed without naming specific individuals. They can emphasize the availability of coaching and development opportunities for those who need support. By doing so, leaders show that the organization is committed to helping everyone succeed, but also serious about maintaining high standards of accountability.

This approach has several benefits:

1. **Reinforces Standards**: It reminds everyone that the organization values high performance and is willing to take necessary actions to maintain it.

2. **Boosts Morale**: High performers feel valued and supported when they see that underperformance is being addressed, preventing frustration and burnout.

3. **Encourages Improvement**: Underperforming individuals are given a clear message that improvement is necessary and are provided with the resources to succeed.

4. **Promotes Fairness**: It creates a sense of fairness and equity, as everyone is held to the same standards and expectations.

I hold a controversial yet necessary viewpoint: Corporate America needs greater transparency regarding accountability and corrective actions. In today's complex business environment, it is crucial for organizations to instill trust and demonstrate their commitment to integrity. While the specifics of an employee's disciplinary measures should remain confidential to respect privacy, it is equally important to communicate that actions are being taken in response to failures or poor leadership.

Transparency in accountability is not about airing every detail but about affirming that there are consequences for actions that do not align with the company's values or performance standards. This can be achieved by ensuring that employees understand that issues are being addressed through direct discussions with those involved and by implementing tangible actions to correct these issues.

Direct discussions about performance problems allow for clear, honest communication and provide an opportunity for affected parties to understand where they went wrong and how they can improve. These conversations should be constructive, aiming to support the individual's growth and development within the organization.

Moreover, implementing tangible corrective actions is essential. This might include additional training, restructuring of responsibilities, or, in some cases, more severe measures. Such actions demonstrate that the organization is serious about maintaining high standards and is committed to continuous improvement.

Both direct communication and concrete actions are vital in promoting a culture of accountability and improvement. When employees see that the company holds everyone to the same standards and takes necessary steps to address issues, it builds a culture of trust and mutual respect. This, in turn, can lead to increased determination, better performance, and a stronger organizational reputation.

That said, I believe that underperforming confidentiality shields should not apply to senior management. Why? Because as leaders of the organization, they are responsible for making critical decisions and driving the organization forward. Laziness, lack of attention to detail, failure to hold others accountable, negligence, and simply not doing their jobs are unacceptable given their position, salary, and privileges. Therefore, they should be exempt from public disclosures of their poor behavior and performance. This does not mean it cannot be done without tact and a sense of professionalism. However, at their level of leadership, they should ideally step up and acknowledge their failures and present their solutions. Their shortcomings should not be something that others need to disclose on their behalf. However, too often, pride and a lack of development into true leaders obstruct this process. And due to our overdeveloped sense of wanting to protect someone's pride, we fail to maintain accountability and transparency.

While the privacy of individual disciplinary actions should be maintained, corporate America must strive for greater transparency in how it handles accountability. By doing so, companies can create a culture that values integrity, encourages improvement, and ultimately achieves better overall performance. And in the end, your high performers will become more loyal to your organization and to you as their leader. When they see accountability and transparency in action, they gain a clear understanding of the challenges and failures the organization faces. By being part of the solution, they will feel more invested in the organization's success. This commitment to open communication and addressing issues head-on will create a culture of trust and continuous improvement, encouraging high performers to stay engaged and motivated.

Overcoming Preconceived Notions as a Leader

As a leader, it's crucial to move beyond your preconceived notions and embrace the principles of followership and empowerment. Effective followership emphasizes the importance of listening to and valuing the contributions of your team members, while empowerment involves giving them the autonomy and confidence to make decisions and share ideas. Recognize that your ideas and firmly held beliefs are not always the best or the only path forward.

Disengagement rapidly spreads when a team senses bias in their leader's response to ideas, discussions, or decisions. Leadership demands breaking free from a rigid mindset and being open to diverse perspectives. Consider how many potential breakthroughs were never voiced due to fear of immediate rejection by decision-makers. Leaders must be constantly vigilant of their biases and preconceptions, as these can stifle growth, advance discontent, and inhibit empowerment.

By leading towards a culture that embraces followership, where team members feel heard and respected, and by empowering them to take the initiative and contribute meaningfully, leaders can unlock the full potential of their teams. This approach drives innovation, enhances engagement, and ultimately leads to greater success. Empowerment not only boosts individual confidence and performance but also creates a more dynamic and resilient team capable of achieving remarkable outcomes.

The key to setting aside preconceived notions lies in self-awareness, openness, and encouraging feedback from those unafraid to speak truthfully. In 2021, when I was in the role of Director, a direct report suggested a new solution they believed would significantly enhance our organization. Initially, I dismissed the suggestion out of hand due to past experiences with similar initiatives, which had not yielded the desired results.

However, I had a strong working relationship with this direct report. They challenged my narrow perspective by presenting detailed data and a well-thought-out plan, which highlighted the potential benefits and addressed the concerns I had based on previous experiences. Their persistence and clarity helped me realize that I might be making a hasty judgment. Going against my now formed methodology of the EmpowerTrust Dynamic.

After reevaluating the proposal and discussing it further, I recognized the potential value in their suggestion. And that I needed to follow their lead. We decided to implement the new solution, and as a result, we achieved a very positive outcome, which significantly improved our division's performance and efficiency.

Incidents like this underscore the importance of surrounding yourself with team members who can—and will—offer their honest perspectives. It highlights the need for leaders to remain open to new ideas, even when past experiences might suggest otherwise. Knowing when to step back and listen to someone else's expertise is a fundamental leadership skill. It nurtures a culture of collaboration and continuous improvement, ultimately driving the organization forward.

Always ask yourself: Are my preconceived notions hindering progress or necessary change? How does this impact my team and the organization? Ask yourself if any of these resonate? And if so, you may went to reflect on any preconceived notations you may be harboring.

1. **Confirmation Bias**: Tendency to seek out information that confirms existing beliefs and ignore contradictory information.

2. **Halo Effect**: Allowing one positive characteristic of an individual to influence overall perception, often leading to an overly favorable view.

3. **Anchoring Bias**: Relying too heavily on the first piece of information encountered (the "anchor") when making decisions.

4. **Overconfidence Bias**: Overestimating one's abilities and the accuracy of their knowledge or predictions.

5. **Status Quo Bias**: Preferring things to stay the same rather than change, even when change might be beneficial.

6. **Recency Bias**: Giving undue weight to the most recent information or experiences.

7. **Groupthink**: Conforming to group opinions and suppressing dissent to maintain harmony, which can stifle innovation and critical thinking.

8. **Hindsight Bias**: Believing, after an event has occurred, that the outcome was predictable and obvious.

9. **Self-Serving Bias**: Attributing successes to personal factors while blaming failures on external factors.

10. **Cognitive Dissonance**: Holding conflicting beliefs or values and rationalizing actions that may be inconsistent with them.

I urge you to discuss openly with your trusted leadership to combat these biases. Address this topic candidly, using examples, even challenging ones, to illustrate how biases may have shaped decisions. Reflect on events that might have contributed to an unapproachable atmosphere. If your organization is experiencing significant turnover, consider whether preconceived notions are a factor.

Expanding on Empowerment Techniques: Agile Leadership and Digital Tools

Enhancing Leadership with Emotional Intelligence: A leader's emotional intelligence—awareness of, control over, and effective expression of emotions, along with the ability to handle interpersonal relationships thoughtfully and empathetically—is vital for empowering others. Leaders with high EI can build trust more effectively, resolve conflicts with sensitivity, and motivate their team members. Moreover, these leaders understand the importance of stepping back to allow their team members to take ownership and grow. Empowerment through emotional intelligence involves recognizing when to step back and let others lead, thereby adopting an environment of trust and autonomy.

Improving your EI starts with active listening, acknowledging the emotional states of your team members, and responding to them with understanding and constructive feedback. By stepping back and giving your team the space to develop their skills and confidence, you create a more resilient and capable team.

Reflection Exercise: Delegating for Growth

1. **Consider a project where more delegation could have been beneficial.** What were your reservations about delegating at the time? Reflect on how stepping back and allowing team members to take on more responsibility could have empowered them and improved the project's outcome.

2. **Identify tasks you're currently managing that could serve as development opportunities for team members.** Outline a plan for transitioning these tasks. Think about how this delegation not only lightens your load but also empowers your team members by giving them a chance to step up and grow.

3. **Recall an instance where your direct involvement might have disrupted the team's workflow.** With hindsight, how could this situation have been approached differently to avoid negative impacts on productivity and morale? Consider how stepping back in similar situations in the future could enhance team empowerment and efficiency.

By integrating emotional intelligence into your leadership style, you not only enhance your ability to connect with and motivate your team but also empower them by providing opportunities for growth and development through thoughtful delegation and stepping back when appropriate.

Final Thoughts

As we conclude this chapter on the EmpowerTrust Dynamic, remember that the essence of leadership is not only about guiding and directing but also about empowering and stepping back. Effective leaders cultivate an environment where their team members can thrive independently, instilling creativity, initiative, and ownership. By avoiding the pitfalls of over-involvement and micromanagement, leaders can create a culture of trust, accountability, and high performance. As you embark on your leadership journey, embrace the principles of followership and empowerment, recognizing that true leadership often involves knowing when to step back and allow others to lead. This balance will not only enhance your team's performance but also build a resilient and innovative organizational culture poised for long-term success.

The highly intelligent leader knows when to lead and more important when to follow.

Chapter 3: Direct Empathetic Communication

Direct Empathetic Communication (DEC) offers a fresh approach to workplace interaction. I define DEC as the ability to communicate honestly and transparently while genuinely caring about the other person's feelings and well-being. This means expressing thoughts and emotions straightforwardly without evasion, and simultaneously understanding the other person's perspective and emotional state. Such communication builds trust and mutual respect, enabling deeper connections. It balances candor with compassion, ensuring honesty does not come at the expense of kindness.

This method can revolutionize workplace communication by promoting straightforward yet compassionate interactions. The goal is to establish a workplace where transparent communication is balanced with a supportive environment. Direct Empathetic Communication is more than just a communication technique; it's a philosophy that can redefine workplace interactions. By embracing DEC, leaders can create an environment of high trust, clear communication, and continuous growth, leading to a more fulfilling workplace.

DEC has the potential to transform any organization. If your company faces stagnation or high employee turnover, consider shifting communication styles, leadership approaches, and philosophical foundations. With workforce dynamics evolving and new generations entering the workplace, DEC principles could prove invaluable. Today's employees often value giving and receiving candid feedback. Embracing this approach aligns well with their expectations and promotes a dynamic environment.

Though DEC may seem challenging, it essentially involves relearning how to communicate openly, honestly, and empathetically. It's easy to point out mistakes, but the real value lies in showing empathy through noble intent and supporting improvements. This approach helps individuals move forward constructively. If underperforming employees are not informed of their shortcomings and continue to believe they meet or exceed expectations, it reflects poorly on your organization and leadership.

When being candid, prepare the other person by saying, " I'd like to have an open and honest discussion about your performance. Please be prepared for some constructive feedback. My aim is to have a productive conversation that fosters growth, not to cause any discomfort." This intertwines empathy with openness, encouraging a more receptive environment for criticism. It also necessitates ongoing feedback, avoiding the surprise of an extensive list of shortcomings. Holding candid conversations without timely communication is essentially dishonest.

Establishing a symbiotic relationship within your organization, where DEC flows naturally, amplifies positive outcomes. Imagine the surge in energy, time savings, and boosted investment returns if we weren't bogged down by misunderstandings and miscommunications. By supporting an environment where directness mixed with empathy is foundational, we create mutual respect and understanding. This enhances collaboration, drives innovation, and improves efficiency. Each interaction becomes more meaningful, reducing the need for prolonged explanations and corrections.

In essence, investing in nurturing empathetic communication not only preserves but multiplies resources. The ripple effects of such an environment can lead to unprecedented synergy and progress, transforming how we work and collaborate.

The Core of Direct Empathetic Communication in Leadership

Direct Empathetic Communication (DEC) is grounded in two core principles: "Intentional Caring" and "Constructive Transparency." This approach involves expressing empathy for employees while engaging in frank discussions about their performance. DEC provides a balanced alternative to ineffective methods such as harsh criticism and non-confrontational avoidance, both of which can harm workplace dynamics.

Harsh criticism is a feedback style delivered bluntly and severely, often pointing out faults without offering constructive guidance. This approach can demoralize employees, damage their confidence, and create a hostile work environment.

Non-confrontational avoidance is a communication style where issues or conflicts are deliberately ignored or sidestepped. By avoiding direct confrontation, this approach can lead to unresolved issues, misunderstandings, and a lack of clear communication, ultimately harming team cohesion and effectiveness.

Passive-aggressive management is a leadership style where negative feelings are indirectly expressed instead of being addressed openly. Manifestations include procrastination, stubbornness, sarcasm, backhanded compliments, and subtle undermining of employees' efforts. This creates an atmosphere of confusion and mistrust, leading to decreased employee morale, productivity, and engagement.

In contrast, DEC redefines directness as compassionate. By shifting from passive-aggressive management to constructive transparency, DEC fosters an environment of mutual respect and understanding. This not only enhances collaboration and teamwork but also drives innovation and efficiency, creating a more dynamic and thriving organization.

Many organizations hesitate to discuss essential business and personal development with underperforming employees, fearing disengagement. However, initial disengagement can turn into full engagement and improved performance if the communication strategy includes a deliberate approach, clear expectations, and candid yet compassionate feedback.

Underperformers, whom other employees almost always notice, can be contagious. Inaction demoralizes competent employees, sometimes driving top performers away. Organizations can encourage a more committed, efficient workforce by proactively addressing performance issues with DEC.

However, it is important to note that DEC is a reciprocal process. It also involves empowering employees to engage their leadership with constructive feedback and empathetic transparency. Such reciprocity emphasizes the importance of creating an environment where leaders are open and empathetic, and employees are encouraged to engage in similar ways.

Empowering employees in this context means fostering a culture where constructive feedback is given and received openly, and transparency is practiced with understanding. This dual focus ensures that communication flows effectively in both directions, creating a workplace atmosphere where employees and leaders build trust, freely exchange ideas, and establish a profound sense of mutual respect. Direct Empathetic Communication is much about nurturing employees' receptive attitudes as it is about leaders modeling those behaviors.

Knowing When to Use Direct Empathetic Communication: Striking the Balance

Direct Empathetic Communication (DEC) is a powerful approach to workplace interaction that emphasizes honesty and empathy. By integrating "Intentional Caring" and "Constructive Transparency," DEC aims to adopt an environment of trust, respect, and collaboration. However, while DEC is beneficial in many scenarios, it's essential to recognize situations where it might not be appropriate and understand how to balance its use effectively.

When to Use DEC:

1. **Routine Performance Feedback:** DEC is particularly effective in providing regular performance feedback. Managers can express appreciation for employees' strengths while addressing areas for improvement in a supportive manner. This ensures that employees feel valued and understood while receiving the guidance they need to grow.

    - **Example:** During a quarterly review, a manager uses DEC to commend an employee's recent project success while constructively discussing areas where they can improve, ensuring the conversation is both honest and empathetic.

2. **Team Collaboration:** DEC enhances teamwork by promoting open dialogue and mutual respect. Encouraging team members to share their ideas and concerns openly furthers a culture of innovation and collaboration.

    - **Example:** In a team meeting, a leader uses DEC to address a conflict between team members, acknowledging each person's perspective and working towards a collaborative solution.

3. **Building Trust:** DEC is crucial for building and maintaining trust within a team. When leaders communicate transparently and show genuine concern for their employees, it creates a foundation of trust that enhances overall team morale and productivity.

    - **Example:** A manager openly discusses upcoming organizational changes, addressing employees' concerns and providing reassurance, thereby strengthening trust within the team.

When DEC Might Not Be Appropriate:

1. **Crisis Situations:** In emergencies, swift and decisive action is required. There may not be time for the nuanced conversations that DEC involves.
   - o **Example:** During a factory equipment malfunction, a manager needs to issue clear and direct instructions to ensure safety, rather than engaging in empathetic dialogue.

2. **Legal or Compliance Issues:** When dealing with legal matters or compliance issues, strict adherence to protocols and confidentiality is paramount, which may limit the application of DEC.
   - o **Example:** If an employee is under investigation for misconduct, the communication should follow legal protocols rather than using DEC, to protect confidentiality and the integrity of the investigation.

3. **Highly Personal Issues:** Personal matters, such as mental health issues, often require professional support rather than managerial intervention through DEC.
   - o **Example:** If an employee is dealing with severe depression, referring them to professional counseling services is more appropriate than a DEC discussion about their performance.

4. **High-Emotion Situations:** When emotions are running high, it might be best to wait until all parties have calmed down before engaging in a DEC conversation.

- o **Example:** If an employee is visibly upset after receiving bad news, allowing them time to process their emotions before discussing performance issues can prevent escalation and ensure a more productive conversation later.

Striking the Balance:

The key to effectively using DEC lies in knowing when to apply it and when to adapt or defer to other communication strategies.

Striking the right balance involves:

1. **Assessing the Situation:** Before engaging in DEC, evaluate the context, urgency, and the emotional state of the individuals involved.

2. **Being Flexible:** Be willing to adapt your communication approach based on the specific needs of the situation. Sometimes, a direct approach is necessary, while other times, a more measured or indirect method might be better.

3. **Prioritizing Empathy and Clarity:** Regardless of the situation, always aim to maintain empathy and clarity. Even in urgent or sensitive scenarios, showing understanding and being clear can help maintain trust and respect.

4. **Continuous Learning:** Encourage ongoing learning and adaptation of communication skills. Understanding cultural nuances, emotional intelligence, and situational dynamics can enhance the effectiveness of DEC and other communication strategies.

By recognizing when to use DEC and when alternative approaches are more appropriate, leaders can create a balanced communication strategy that fosters a positive and productive workplace environment.

The Impact of Direct Empathetic Communication

Direct Empathetic Communication can have a profound impact, leading to:

- **Enhanced Team Performance:** Clear, honest feedback significantly improves productivity and work quality.

- **Personal Growth:** Employees receive constructive feedback that aids their personal and professional development.

- **Improved Member/Customer Services:** Effective internal communication enables better, more empathetic member/customer services.

- **Trust:** Trust is fundamental in candid interactions. Leaders and team members must trust each other to speak and receive the truth. The impact of being able to develop an open environment is trust.

In my career, I have developed Direct Empathetic Communication (DEC) with various individuals, from my direct reports to my peers and leadership. While it can be challenging, I am consistently candid in my conversations and transparent about my intentions to be so. This approach brings a sense of authenticity that was previously lacking in my leadership style and professional interactions.

Since committing to DEC, many of my direct reports have become more authentic with me, breaking away from the "you're my boss" mentality. We can have direct, yet positive and empathetic, communications. This allows us to get to the heart of issues quickly, engage in difficult but productive discussions, and cover a lot of ground efficiently.

The best part is that my team knows what to expect from me. This predictability reduces the emotional impact of direct communications. We can easily transition from difficult professional discussions to personal conversations, such as asking about our families. This shows that we care about more than just the job at hand and have a genuine interest in each other's well-being. By understanding and adopting this balance, we create a supportive and dynamic workplace where both professional and personal aspects are valued. The results? Our production, agility, and ability to navigate tough situations have improved tenfold. The clarity and openness in our communication enable us to respond quickly and effectively to changing circumstances. When we face challenges, my team understands the importance of following directions promptly, knowing that our usual open communication will resume as soon as possible.

This balance between directive leadership in critical moments and our standard empathetic, transparent communication has made us a more resilient and cohesive team. We are better equipped to handle adversity, and our enhanced communication has led to greater productivity and a stronger sense of camaraderie.

Embracing DEC has transformed our work environment. It has set the foundation for authentic relationships, increased efficiency, and has continued to further a culture of trust and mutual respect. This approach not only benefits our professional interactions but also enriches our personal connections, making our workplace a more dynamic and fulfilling space for everyone involved.

Implementing Direct Empathetic Communication

Implementing Direct Empathetic Communication (DEC) within an organization requires careful planning and consistent effort. Here are key steps to effectively integrate this approach into your workplace culture:

Setting the Stage

- **Preparing the Team:**

- o **Host an Initial Meeting:** Hold a meeting to introduce the DEC concept, explaining its principles and benefits. Provide real-life examples of how DEC can positively impact the workplace.

  - o **Create a DEC Guide:** Develop a simple guide or handbook outlining the expectations and practices associated with DEC. Distribute this to all team members to ensure clarity and consistency.

Creating a Safe Environment

- **Fostering Openness:**

  - o **Establish Ground Rules:** Set clear ground rules for DEC discussions to ensure everyone feels safe and respected. Include guidelines on listening, feedback, and confidentiality.

  - o **Regular Check-ins:** Schedule regular check-ins to reinforce the importance of open communication and address any concerns or questions about the DEC process.

Starting Small

- **Gradual Implementation:**

  - o **Pilot Programs:** Start with a pilot program involving a small group or department. Monitor the process, gather feedback, and make necessary adjustments before scaling up.

  - o **Mentorship:** Pair new adopters of DEC with experienced mentors who can guide them through the process and provide support.

Leading by Example

- **Modeling Behavior:**
    - **Public Acknowledgment:** Recognize and publicly acknowledge when team members effectively use DEC, reinforcing its value and encouraging others to follow suit.
    - **Personal Reflection:** Share your own experiences and reflections on using DEC, demonstrating transparency and a commitment to continuous improvement.

Training and Education

- **Building Skills:**
    - **Interactive Workshops:** Organize interactive workshops that include role-playing exercises to help team members practice DEC in a safe and supportive environment.
    - **Online Resources:** Provide access to online resources, such as articles, videos, and e-courses, that team members can use to further develop their DEC skills.

Encouraging Feedback

- **Valuing Input:**
    - **Feedback Channels:** Establish multiple channels for feedback, such as suggestion boxes, online forms, and regular one-on-one meetings, to make it easy for employees to share their thoughts.
    - **Feedback Training:** Offer training on how to give and receive feedback effectively, emphasizing the role of empathy and constructive criticism.

Addressing Challenges

- **Providing Support:**
    - **Coaching Sessions:** Schedule regular coaching sessions for individuals who struggle with DEC, offering personalized advice and strategies to help them improve.
    - **Peer Support Groups:** Create peer support groups where team members can discuss their experiences with DEC and learn from each other.

Regular Check-ins and Adjustments

- **Continuous Improvement:**
    - **Feedback Surveys:** Conduct regular surveys to assess the effectiveness of DEC implementation and gather suggestions for improvement.
    - **Adjustment Meetings:** Hold periodic meetings to review DEC practices, discuss what is working, and identify areas that need adjustment.

Celebrating Successes

- **Recognizing Achievements:**
    - **Success Stories:** Share success stories and case studies within the organization to highlight the positive impact of DEC.

Integrating DEC into Organizational Practices

- **Embedding in Culture:**
    - **DEC in Reviews:** Incorporate DEC principles into performance review processes, ensuring that feedback is both direct and empathetic.

- **Policy Inclusion:** Include DEC guidelines in organizational policies and employee handbooks to reinforce its importance.

What Does Honesty and Empathy Look Like in Practice?

Honesty in Practice:

- **Clear Communication:** Always articulate your thoughts and feedback clearly and straightforwardly. Avoid vague or ambiguous language that can lead to misunderstandings. Ask if they understand. And have empathy to encourage that, if they don't, to please ask and we will work together.

- **Transparency:** Share information openly, including the reasons behind decisions and any relevant context. This builds trust and ensures everyone is on the same page.

- **Accountability:** Own up to your mistakes and encourage others to do the same. This fosters a culture of integrity and continuous improvement.

Empathy in Practice:

- **Active Listening:** Pay close attention to what others are saying without interruption. Show that you value their input by responding thoughtfully and acknowledging their feelings.

- **Understanding Perspectives:** Make an effort to understand the viewpoints and emotional states of your colleagues. This can involve asking questions and expressing genuine interest in their experiences.

- **Support and Encouragement:** Offer support and positive reinforcement, especially when delivering constructive feedback. Highlight strengths and achievements alongside areas for improvement to maintain morale and motivation.

Implementing Direct Empathetic Communication is a transformative process that requires dedication and intentionality. By setting the stage, creating a safe environment, starting small, leading by example, providing training, encouraging feedback, and addressing challenges, you can successfully integrate DEC into your organization. The result is a more transparent, empathetic, and productive workplace where open communication and mutual respect are the norms.

Direct Empathetic Communication in Action: A Real-World Perspective

Understanding that the success of Direct Empathetic Communication hinges on practical implementation, a mid-sized financial services firm, for example, launched a comprehensive training program titled "Empathy and Transparency in Leadership." The program included interactive modules on active listening, constructive feedback, and emotional intelligence, coupled with role-playing exercises that allowed participants to practice new skills in real-life scenarios. Post-training surveys revealed a remarkable improvement in communication clarity and team cohesion, evidencing the program's impact.

Navigating the Challenges: A Balanced Approach

While the benefits of Direct Empathetic Communication are manifold, it's not without its challenges. A common concern among managers is misinterpreting empathy as a lack of firmness or the inability to make tough decisions. To address this, a leading healthcare provider introduced a segment in their leadership development program titled "Empathy with Boundaries." This segment focused on how leaders balance showing genuine concern and enforcing necessary professional boundaries. This approach helped clarify that empathy does not equate to leniency but is a strategic tool for adopting a supportive yet high-performing work environment.

INTERMISSION – This is a long chapter, and we have already covered a lot of information. Now may be a good time for a quick intermission to let what we have covered digest for a bit.

If your intermission was over a day or two here is a quick recap of what the chapter covered to this point:

> Direct Empathetic Communication (DEC) redefines workplace interaction by balancing honesty with empathy, promoting transparent and caring communication. DEC involves expressing thoughts and emotions straightforwardly while understanding others' perspectives and emotional states, thereby building trust and mutual respect. This approach fosters a supportive environment, enhancing collaboration, innovation, and efficiency. DEC is more than a communication technique; it's a philosophy that can revolutionize organizational dynamics, especially in addressing performance issues and preventing misunderstandings. It advocates for regular, candid feedback intertwined with empathy, avoiding harsh criticism or non-confrontational avoidance, which can harm workplace morale. DEC also empowers employees to give and receive feedback openly, fostering a culture of mutual respect and continuous improvement. While beneficial in many scenarios, DEC's application should be balanced with other communication strategies, especially in emergencies, legal matters, or highly emotional situations. Implementing DEC involves careful planning, setting clear guidelines, fostering openness, starting small, leading by example, and providing ongoing training and support. This transformative approach enhances team performance, personal growth, and trust, creating a more dynamic and fulfilling workplace.

A Personal Journey to Empathetic Leadership

Now let's outline a personal example of practical application:

John, a project manager at a multinational FinTech firm, shares his transformative journey of integrating Direct Empathetic Communication (DEC) into his leadership style. Initially skeptical, John feared that a focus on empathy might undermine his authority and lead to a lack of discipline and respect among his team. He worried that being too open and understanding would make him seem weak or indecisive.

John's perspective began to shift after he attended a workshop on DEC. The workshop, designed to highlight the balance between empathy and effective leadership, introduced him to the principles of Intentional Caring and Constructive Transparency. John learned that empathy and authority are not mutually exclusive; rather, they can complement each other to create a more cohesive and motivated team.

Armed with new insights, John decided to experiment with more open and empathetic communication with his team. He began by:

- **Active Listening:** John made a conscious effort to listen more actively during team meetings, ensuring that every team member had the opportunity to voice their thoughts and concerns. He asked follow-up questions to show genuine interest and understanding.

- **Transparency:** John started sharing more about the decision-making processes and the rationale behind certain project strategies. He openly discussed challenges the team faced and invited input on potential solutions.

- **Acknowledging Emotions:** John became more attentive to the emotional states of his team members. When someone appeared stressed or frustrated, he took the time to address these feelings directly, offering support and understanding.

The results of these changes were transformative. John's team began to exhibit several positive changes:

- **Increased Proactivity:** Team members became more proactive in addressing project challenges. They felt empowered to take the initiative, knowing that their input would be valued and respected. This led to quicker problem-solving and more efficient project management.

- **Enhanced Innovation:** With a more open communication environment, team members felt comfortable sharing innovative ideas. The fear of judgment diminished, leading to a surge in creativity and new approaches to engineering problems.

- **Stronger Trust and Collaboration:** The team developed a deeper sense of trust and collaboration. Knowing that John genuinely cared about their well-being and valued their contributions, team members were more willing to support each other and work together towards common goals.

- **Improved Morale and Engagement:** Overall morale improved as team members felt heard and appreciated. This boosted engagement and commitment to their work, leading to higher productivity and job satisfaction.

Reflecting on his journey, John realized that embracing vulnerability and empathy did not weaken his authority; instead, it strengthened his leadership. By showing that he was willing to listen and understand, John earned greater respect and loyalty from his team. The balance of honesty and empathy cultivated an environment where team members felt safe to express themselves and contribute fully.

The long-term benefits of implementing DEC were evident in several areas:

- **Retention:** The supportive and open culture John cultivated helped retain top talent. Team members were less likely to seek opportunities elsewhere, knowing they were in a positive and growth-oriented environment.

- **Reputation:** John's success with DEC garnered attention within the firm, setting a benchmark for other managers. His department became known for its high performance and innovative solutions, enhancing his reputation as a capable and empathetic leader.

- **Personal Growth:** On a personal level, John experienced significant growth. He became more self-aware and emotionally intelligent, skills that not only improved his professional life but also enriched his personal relationships.

John's story is a testament to the power of vulnerability and empathy in building trust and driving performance. By integrating Direct Empathetic Communication into his leadership style, he transformed his team's dynamics, fostering an environment of innovation, trust, and high performance. John's journey illustrates that empathy, far from undermining authority, can be a critical component of effective and inspirational leadership.

Mitigating the Risks of Direct Empathetic Communication

Implementing Direct Empathetic Communication (DEC) is a powerful strategy for supporting a culture of openness and mutual respect. However, it is essential to navigate the potential risks carefully to maintain a positive and productive environment.

The Dangers of Brutal Honesty: Brutally honest opinions, without the balance of empathy, can lead to frustration, chaos, or negativity within a team. When employees feel that their ideas and feedback are not valued or heard, they may become disengaged and less likely to contribute in the future. Effective DEC requires a nuanced approach to ensure that honesty is delivered with care and consideration for others' feelings.

Understanding Your Audience: A key aspect of successful DEC is knowing your audience. Understanding the leadership level, personality style, and communication preferences of individuals or teams is critical when adopting more candid and open communication. DEC is not a one-size-fits-all method; it requires ongoing adjustment and sensitivity to the unique dynamics of each group.

Embracing Feedback Without Guaranteeing Implementation: DEC does not mean that all feedback or ideas will be implemented. Instead, it focuses on creating an environment where feedback is welcomed and valued. When leaders make decisions, it is crucial for the team to unite and move forward together, even if not all ideas are adopted. Practicing DEC means becoming comfortable with this process and fostering a culture where feedback is seen as a constructive part of decision-making.

Encouraging Open Dialogue: As a leader, I encourage my team to openly challenge my ideas and provide direct feedback on my leadership style or decision-making processes. I value their perspectives and rely on their insights to improve our collective performance. However, it is also essential to establish that, ultimately, decisions need to be made, and the team must support these decisions to ensure progress.

Handling Disappointment and Anger: When feedback or ideas are not embraced, it is natural for team members to feel disappointed. However, it is crucial to differentiate between disappointment and anger. Disappointment indicates a healthy response to an outcome, while anger might suggest unresolved issues or unclear expectations.

To mitigate negative reactions, it is vital to provide follow-up and follow-through. This involves explaining why certain feedback or ideas were not implemented, ensuring that team members understand the rationale behind decisions. By maintaining transparency and offering clear explanations, leaders can reinforce an environment of mutual respect where everyone feels heard.

Mitigating the risks associated with Direct Empathetic Communication requires a careful and thoughtful approach. By balancing honesty with empathy, understanding your audience, and encouraging an environment where feedback is valued but not always implemented, you can maintain engagement and unity within your team. Encouraging open dialogue and addressing disappointment with clarity and transparency are crucial steps in building a resilient and collaborative work environment.

The Path Forward

Implementing DEC is not without its challenges, but the rewards can be of epic proportions. As you move forward, consider how the principles of DEC can be applied to enhance both followership and leadership within your organization. Encourage your team to embrace both giving and receiving feedback with empathy and clarity. Create spaces where open dialogue is not only accepted but expected.

Incorporating DEC into your practices will pave the way for a more dynamic, resilient, and high-performing organization. As leaders, by demonstrating empathy and transparency, we set the stage for followers to rise, contribute meaningfully, and drive collective success.

Direct Empathetic Communication is a cornerstone of effective followership and leadership. By adopting DEC, leaders can cultivate a culture of openness and respect, empowering their teams to achieve greater heights. Remember, the journey of leadership is a continuous one, and DEC is a powerful tool that can guide you and your team towards a future of shared success and mutual growth.

Finally – Our Conclusion

As we conclude this chapter on Direct Empathetic Communication (DEC), it is essential to reflect on its profound impact on organizational culture and leadership effectiveness. By integrating DEC into everyday interactions, leaders can help support and develop an environment of trust, respect, and innovation. The principles of DEC are not merely about improving communication but about transforming relationships and building a stronger, more cohesive team.

The journey through DEC reveals that empathy and honesty, when balanced correctly, can lead to significant improvements in team engagement, productivity, and overall morale. Leaders who embrace this approach not only enhance their effectiveness but also create a culture where every team member feels valued and heard.

Chapter 4: Having Fun

Being a successful leader and follower requires having some fun. While it's true that few of us have the type of jobs that make us want to leap out of bed every morning and make a mad dash for the office, having fun can make the working environment interesting, lively, and engaging.

Organization-wide activities like ugly sweater contests, trivia, and other items typically driven by HR, marketing, or sales can be enjoyable. The type of fun I focus on in this chapter is a bit more siloed.

If you're a follower and your leader is trying to have fun with something, support it! Get in on the action. Don't be a downer when someone is genuinely trying to make things pleasant. Not participating, only giving 50%, not allowing yourself to enjoy the moment, glued to your phone, or chatting with your workers behind the scenes about how this is not going well are all signs that you may need to take a step back and determine if you are practicing followership.

With that said, if your leader is consistently trying things that are backfiring, talk to your leader about it. They will thank you for it, and the team will thank you. Your leader may even come up with some alternatives that everyone truly enjoys.

Before we get into talking about fun, it's important to note that it can't be forced, fun can be a disaster if it's done the wrong way!

Once, I reported to a technically brilliant but socially awkward leader. Putting this person in a leadership role was a misstep; unfortunately, at the time, brilliance in our field and managing others went hand in hand. Every time this person tried to be funny or engage in icebreakers or other poorly thought-out types of fun, they failed. Out came the fake laughs. Even more regrettably, this person had no idea it was going wrong. The fake laughs didn't faze them, and the people involved felt unable to say that his schemes were simply not going well.

Imagine the scene for a moment: It's a Monday morning, and the team is gathered in the conference room. This awkward leader, John, steps up with an eager smile, holding a stack of cards. "Today, we're going to start with a fun game!" he announces, his voice brimming with enthusiasm that isn't quite reciprocated by the room. The game is a classic icebreaker – "Two Truths and a Lie." John goes first, sharing his three statements. As he reveals the lie, he bursts into laughter, looking expectantly around the room. The team members exchange glances, offering polite chuckles and forced smiles, their discomfort palpable. The room feels tense, the forced joviality creating an undercurrent of unease.

Every attempt at humor or team bonding seems to fall flat, creating a barrier between John and his team. The more he tries, the more strained the interactions become. The team feels the pressure to play along, masking their true feelings behind insincere laughter.

Until I came along, that is. The first time I mentioned the problem to my leader, John, was awkward and difficult, as coaching up often is. I reminded myself that he's a person, just like me. He puts his pants on like I do, one leg at a time. Once I explained that I, to the depths of my being, wanted to help, the awkwardness melted away. A shift began.

I approached John privately, choosing my words carefully. "John, I've noticed that the team doesn't seem to be responding well to the icebreakers," I began, my tone gentle yet direct. He looked surprised but didn't interrupt. "I think they're feeling pressured to laugh, which makes the whole experience less enjoyable for everyone, including you."

John's face reddened slightly, but he nodded slowly. "I didn't realize," he admitted. "I just want to connect with them."

I could see his sincerity, and it encouraged me. "Maybe we could try a different approach," I suggested. "Something more organic, where everyone feels comfortable."

We brainstormed together, coming up with activities that were more in tune with the team's interests. Instead of structured Googled icebreakers, we introduced casual coffee chats and team lunches where conversations could flow naturally. John also started sharing personal stories, not as a forced exercise but as genuine moments of connection.

The change was remarkable. Real laughter began to echo in the office, replacing the hollow sound of fake chuckles. Team members opened up, sharing their own stories and jokes. The atmosphere lightened, supporting deeper relationships and a sense of camaraderie that hadn't been there before.

The tangible outcomes were evident. The team's morale improved, and with it, their productivity. Projects moved forward with a newfound energy, collaboration became more fluid, and even during stressful times, the team could find moments of genuine fun to keep spirits high. John's leadership style evolved, becoming more inclusive and empathetic. He learned to read the room, understanding when to inject humor and when to keep things serious.

In essence, the coaching not only helped John become a better leader but also transformed the team's dynamic. The no longer "forced, fun", replaced with realism gave way to real enjoyment, creating an environment where everyone could thrive both professionally and personally.

Understanding Your Team and Balancing Fun

Before diving into fun activities, it's essential to understand your team's preferences. Taking the time to conduct a simple survey or have informal discussions can provide valuable insights into what types of activities will genuinely resonate with everyone. Open communication not only ensures that the activities you plan will be enjoyable but also makes your team feel heard and valued.

Start with small, low-stakes activities to build comfort and camaraderie. For instance, introduce a "Fun Fact Friday" where team members can share unique tidbits about themselves. This simple yet effective exercise can create personal connections without significantly disrupting the workflow. Another idea could be a monthly themed dress-up day, where everyone gets a chance to express their creativity and have a good laugh together.

As you introduce these activities, be mindful of the work environment and individual preferences. Not everyone may feel comfortable participating in certain activities, so it's important to create an inclusive atmosphere. Consider having a variety of activities that cater to different interests – perhaps a mix of physical activities, like a lunchtime walking group, and more relaxed options, like a puzzle corner in the break room.

Maintaining a balance between fun and productivity is crucial. Clearly define the boundaries between work time and relaxation time. Set specific times for fun activities, such as during lunch breaks or at the end of the workday, to ensure they don't interfere with important tasks. This approach not only respects the workplace but also enhances the overall enjoyment of it.

Regularly check in with your team to gather feedback on the activities and make adjustments as needed. This ongoing dialogue helps to keep the fun elements fresh and relevant. Remember, a happy team is a productive team, and thoughtfully incorporating fun into the workplace can create a more harmonious and engaging environment.

Integrating fun at work is not just about boosting morale – it's about raising a positive, inclusive culture where everyone feels connected and motivated. By understanding your team's preferences, starting small, and maintaining a clear boundary between work and play, you can create a workplace where productivity and enjoyment go hand in hand.

Diversity of Fun: Expanded Strategies

To effectively integrate fun into the workplace, it's beneficial to explore a variety of strategies that cater to different interests and dynamics within your team. Diversifying the types of activities not only keeps things fresh but also ensures that everyone can find something they enjoy and can engage with. Here are some creative and innovative ideas to consider:

- **Creative Brainstorming Sessions**: Transform routine brainstorming sessions into dynamic and invigorating activities by changing the environment. Hosting these sessions in a local park, café, or even a quiet garden can provide a fresh perspective and inspire creativity. The change in scenery helps break the monotony of the usual meeting rooms and can lead to more innovative ideas. Consider bringing in some snacks or refreshments to make the session even more enjoyable and relaxed.

- **Skill-Sharing Workshops**: Encourage team members to lead short, informal workshops where they share a skill or hobby, they are passionate about. These workshops can range from cooking classes and photography lessons to coding tutorials or even yoga sessions. Not only does this add variety to the workday, but it also promotes continuous learning and personal development. Additionally, it provides an opportunity for team members to practice public speaking in a supportive, low-stakes environment, which can boost their confidence and presentation skills.

- **Virtual Reality (VR) Meetings**: Leverage the latest VR technology to conduct meetings in a virtual space designed for relaxation or creativity. This innovative approach can make the work environment more engaging, especially for remote teams who might miss the sense of presence that in-person meetings offer. In a VR setting, you can design meeting rooms that look like serene beaches, futuristic offices, or cozy cabins, making the experience more enjoyable. VR meetings can also include interactive elements such as virtual whiteboards and 3D models to enhance collaboration.

By incorporating these diverse strategies, you can create a more vibrant and inclusive workplace where fun and productivity go hand in hand. These activities not only enhance team cohesion but also contribute to a more dynamic and engaging work environment, ultimately fostering greater job satisfaction and innovation.

Research and Data: Fun Evidence

Recent studies show that companies that regularly engage in team-building activities report a 24% higher employee satisfaction rate. Incorporating fun into the workplace has also been linked to a 21% increase in productivity, according to a 2022 report by the Global Workplace Analytics Institute. These statistics highlight the tangible benefits of integrating fun into professional environments.

Global Workplace Analytics. (2022). *State of Remote Work 2022.* Retrieved from https://globalworkplaceanalytics.com/downloads/state-of-remote-work-2022

Ok, Back to the Fun

As a leader, incorporating fun into your environment cannot be a once-a-quarter thing. Fun shouldn't happen only when Human Resources reviews their annual survey or when it's time to provide feedback. Fun must be something that you, as the leader, try to encourage regularly. Cultivating fun doesn't require all out on a planned adventure, though. Creating more fun can be as simple as participating in water cooler talk and getting to know everyone on the team as a person—learn about their interests, their hobbies, and their passions outside of work.

I'm not unique in encouraging this. Almost every book on leadership stresses the importance of walking around and getting to know the team. Yet, I see so many managers, directors, vice presidents, C-suite executives, and other leaders who skip this simple, straightforward task that creates fun.

When people see that you are a person, it will enable positivity. You don't have to be a prominent scary leader—you can be a person other people enjoy talking to.

As a leader, I try to walk about each morning, afternoon, and evening. My job is to encourage, ask about people's days, know about their lives, and joke with them. Talk to them, vent, grieve, and laugh with them.

Knowing your audience is critical. You can't just jump in, crack a joke, or ask a question, especially if you already have the reputation of being a bit standoffish or intimidating. You have to get to know people and allow relationships to develop over time. Being intentional about fun doesn't mean forcing it. However, you can intentionally position yourself to interact casually with your teams, partner with people on projects, and walk around saying hello in the morning.

Start by sharing personal things about your life or asking a simple question. Getting to know people and having fun conversations should be low-stakes!

I frequently asked my senior direct reports about their lives when they were younger, asking about their families, and what they did on the weekends. Being the boss doesn't mean I'm not also an interested colleague. Valuing people's professional and personal experiences creates a bond and a positive, fun atmosphere that shows we are not all corporate drones.

Of Course, the Arranged Events are Critical, too!

Get-togethers, games, and group outings are essential for team morale. Do us all a favor, though. Unless it's an organization-wide event like a giant Christmas party, ensure the get-togethers are during the working day. People have lives and will be more engaged in your efforts if you haven't impacted their precious time outside the office.

You can also incorporate fun into the required boring events of the workday. We all have the humdrum features of our daily, weekly, monthly, or annual duties. I am not saying not to take them seriously, but you can mix a little bit of fun into things while also easing the difficulty of the boring event.

Take annual training, for example—the same old PowerPoint or video that everyone has had to watch since 1995. We often ask teams to complete these efforts independently. No matter who you are—a part-time teller or the CEO—parts of these annual training courses are mind-numbing. On top of that, we all know that 75% or more of our team members retain less than 25% of the materials.

Take something like Information Security Annual Training and Awareness, a phrase that might have put you to sleep all by itself. I work in technology, and when I learn that this training is upon us, my heart sinks. I start scrolling through my priority list, looking for anything else I can do. It's not that I don't think the training is important, because it is. Unfortunately, the delivery, the quality of information, and the bizarre tests at the end leave much to be desired.

We all know I'm not the only one having that reaction. So how do we change it? Easy! As the leader, figure out how to make boring tasks fun.

As the leader, you will need to invest time and energy in finding ways to make boring tasks genuinely engaging. As a follower, consider the alternative when you see your leader trying to increase enjoyment for a particular activity.

Let's use the security training example to illustrate how you can accomplish this. Instead of having everyone sit alone at their desks feeling bored, turn the annual training session into a group activity—an easy, fun, interactive session.

You can facilitate the event or bring in a facilitator with a sense of humor, character, and the ability to be animated. Play upbeat music and offer a bunch of small prizes like candy and tootsie rolls, with a large prize like an extra PTO day for the person with the most candy. The most significant points are engagement and speed. It can't be a four-hour lecture; it has to be a 45-minute event that is quick, fun, and memorable.

Trivia Challenge

Objective:

- **Question Preparation:** Develop a set of trivia questions covering various topics related to your industry. For example, if you're at a credit union, this might include financial regulations, credit union history, current tech trends in finance (like mobile banking or cybersecurity), and questions specific to your services and policies.

- **Platform Choice:** Decide if the game will be conducted in person or virtually. Use a digital platform (like Kahoot! or Quizizz) for an interactive experience, especially if employees are remote.

- **Team Formation:** Create teams, mixing departments to encourage cross-functional engagement. Smaller teams (3-4 members) usually work best for trivia games.

How to Play:

- **Game Rounds:** Organize the game into multiple rounds, each focusing on a different category (e.g., Credit Union History, Tech Innovations, Financial Laws).

- **Answering Questions:** Teams answer questions within a set time limit. Points are awarded for correct answers, with potential bonus points for speed or difficulty.

- **Interactive Elements:** Include interactive elements like challenge questions, where teams can challenge others on specific questions for extra points.

- **Final Round:** Have a high-stakes final round with more difficult questions. High-stakes questions could include scenarios that require teams to apply their knowledge to hypothetical situations.

Post-Game:

- **Debrief and Learn:** After the game, have a session to discuss the correct answers and provide additional insights or information to reinforce the learning.

- **Reward and Recognize:** Offer small prizes or recognition for the winning team and acknowledge all participants for their involvement and learning.

This game tests and reinforces employees' knowledge and encourages team building and inter-departmental communication in a fun and competitive environment.

If trivia or games aren't quite your thing, another equally effective approach exists. Being genuine and straightforward with your team can achieve powerful results. The fun might not be as flashy, but your team will be more engaged. For example, you can organize a meeting where you candidly acknowledge the reluctance that often accompanies mandatory training sessions. Address the elephant in the room: the redundancy and monotony of such training can be frustrating. However, pivot to emphasize the significance of why you're all there. Request their focused attention for 30-45 minutes to collaboratively navigate through the material. Instead of delivering a monologue, adopt a round-table discussion where an open, classroom-style dialogue prevails.

Here is how you could setup a classroom-style dialogue setting:

Planning the Session

- **Define the Objective:** Clearly outline what you want to achieve with the session. This could be discussing new technologies in your industry, addressing customer service strategies, or exploring regulatory changes.
- **Select a Topic:** Choose a relevant and engaging topic for your audience. It should be broad enough to allow diverse opinions but specific enough to remain focused.
- **Prepare Background Material:** Provide participants with any necessary reading or resources in advance. This could

include articles, case studies, or internal documents that will inform the discussion.

Setting Up the Environment

- **Arrange the Room:** Set the room in a circular or U-shaped layout to facilitate an open discussion. Ensure everyone has a clear line of sight to everyone else.

- **Technology Setup:** If needed, set up technology for presentations, video conferencing (for remote participants), or real-time polling.

- **Establish Ground Rules:** At the beginning of the session, establish ground rules for discussion. Encourage respect for differing opinions, active listening, and a no-interruption policy when someone is speaking.

Conducting the Session

- **Introduction:** Introduce the topic and the session's objectives briefly. Highlight why the topic is essential for the participants.

- **Facilitation:** Your role as the facilitator is to guide the discussion, encourage participation, and keep the conversation on track. Ask open-ended questions to stimulate discussion.

- **Encourage Participation:** Ensure everyone has a chance to speak. You can directly invite quieter members to share their thoughts.

- **Manage Dynamics:** Be attentive to group dynamics. If someone dominates the conversation, gently steer the discussion to include others. If a topic becomes contentious, drive it back to constructive dialogue.

- **Use of Real-life Examples:** Encourage participants to relate discussion points to their experiences. This makes the discussion more relatable and practical.

Concluding the Session

- **Summarize Key Points:** At the end of the session, summarize the key points or takeaways. This recap helps reinforce the learning.
- **Feedback and Reflection:** Ask participants about the session and what they learned. This can be done verbally or through a quick written survey.
- **Follow-up Actions:** Discuss any follow-up actions or further reading if applicable. This could include exploring a topic in more detail or implementing new ideas in the workplace.

Remember, the success of a round table discussion largely depends on creating an atmosphere of openness and mutual respect. Encouraging diverse viewpoints and fostering a comfortable sharing environment will lead to a more enriching and educational experience.

Embracing Fun Work Beyond Activities

Creating fun isn't all about scheduling enjoyable activities, laughter, and jokes—it's rarely about that at all. Fortunately, we can define fun in many ways. For instance, I find completing monthly reports tedious. Yet, engaging in projects, unraveling complex problems, drafting communications to the organization, and energizing others about new initiatives bring me joy and a type of fun.

The key is finding balance. Each of us has tasks we dread and those we consider fun. Identifying these enjoyable elements within our teams and leveraging them while balancing the pleasant with the less enjoyable can foster engagement, prevent burnout, and, most importantly, instill a sense of accomplishment.

Early in my career, I realized that I enjoyed synthesizing complex data into clean, readable reports. Crafting a concise executive summary that outlined the purpose, interpreted the data, reviewed options, and concluded with a recommended direction was mentally taxing yet exhilarating. Upon submitting that executive summary, I felt immense pride and accomplishment. It was a triple win, satisfying my intellectual curiosity, contributing meaningful insights, and receiving recognition for my work. However, this often came at a cost: 5 o'clock rolled around, and I would realize I hadn't completed my day-to-day tasks. Time management still matters, enhance the balance of fun. You must find what does bring you joy while self-managing those not so exciting tasks.

Incorporating fun into work isn't about distracting us from our responsibilities; it's about blending those responsibilities with elements that resonate with us and our team members. Identifying and integrating the fun can transform even the most mundane tasks into opportunities for engagement. The challenge lies in recognizing these opportunities and applying them, making the workplace into a place where work becomes enjoyable.

Addressing Potential Challenges

Think back to the example I shared at the start of the chapter. My leader was trying to make work fun—and it was backfiring. Fun isn't always easy, and it's important to understand the challenges up front so you can address them effectively.

- **Resistance from Team Members:** Address skepticism by starting with voluntary participation and sharing success stories from other organizations.
- **Logistical Obstacles:** Virtual activities can be an excellent alternative for teams facing logistical challenges. Online escape rooms and multiplayer games can offer a

shared fun experience without the need for physical presence.

- **Balancing Diversity:** Ensure activities are inclusive and considerate of all team members' backgrounds and preferences. Offering multiple activities can help meet diverse interests and physical abilities.

The Lasting Impact of Fun in the Workplace

Whether you're casually walking around to engage your team, thoughtfully planning team-building activities, facilitating opportunities for followers to immerse themselves in tasks they find enjoyable, or discovering your sources of workplace joy, the underlying message is clear: a little fun can make a significant difference in the workplace.

Engaging with people informally breaks down barriers and allows you to understand their motivations, challenges, and what brings them joy at work. This understanding is crucial in creating an environment where each team member feels valued and understood.

When it comes to planning activities, remember that you're not just taking a break from work. Well-planned activities advance a sense of community, encourage collaboration, and provide a platform for creative expression. These activities can be catalysts for team bonding and serve as informal settings for innovation.

Empowering your team members to engage in tasks they find fun, and fulfilling is perhaps one of the most effective ways to boost morale and productivity. When people are passionate about their work, they perform better, and the workplace dynamic improves.

Finding your fun tasks is equally important. As a leader and a follower, your attitude toward work can set the tone for the entire team. Visibly enjoying and taking pride in your work can inspire others to find joy in their own tasks.

As a follower, communicate what you find enjoyable about your work. Managers can't always cater to individual preferences, but making your interests known can have a significant impact. Exchanging preferences opens the door to opportunities; what you find enjoyable might be something your manager dislikes, and vice versa. Sharing your interests plants a seed that could grow into more enjoyable tasks.

A little fun goes a long way in building a positive workplace culture, enhancing employee satisfaction and engagement, and ultimately, driving organizational success. By valuing and integrating fun into our daily work lives, we enrich our experiences and contribute to a more vibrant, productive, and fulfilling workplace for everyone. It doesn't have to be grand or expensive. Simple is often safe.

And remember, walk around and engage with team members. If your team is fully remote, use chat to ask about their day or weekend. Or pop in for 5-10 minutes for a quick coffee break. It might be awkward for the receiver at first. So, invest time in planning your 5-10 virtual coffee drop in. A great topic might be even to address the awkwardness of this first coffee session, but combat that by expressing your true intention. To get to know your teammates, create a little fun, and generally create some intentional connections.

Chapter 5: Self-Care as Leaders and Followers

In the relentless pursuit of leadership and followership, amid the whirlwind of duties and the intense pressure to perform, a vital element often falls by the wayside: self-care. This oversight is not due to a lack of understanding or undervaluing our well-being. Neglecting self-care often emerges from the mistaken belief that constant activity and sacrifice are the sole paths to success. In a high-stakes environment, leaders and followers may inadvertently neglect the practices that sustain their energy, focus, and capacity for innovation. The truth is that prioritizing well-being isn't a luxury—it's an essential cornerstone of sustained success.

Neglecting self-care undermines the promise of effective leadership and followership. Can you relate to any of these?

- **Ignoring Physical Health:**
    - Skipping exercise, unhealthy eating, insufficient sleep, ignoring illness.

- **Neglecting Mental Health:**
    - Avoiding stress management, working excessively, no breaks or vacations.
- **Overlooking Emotional Well-being:**
    - Suppressing emotions, neglecting hobbies, personal relationships, and boundaries.
- **Neglecting Professional Development:**
    - Skipping learning opportunities, avoiding feedback, and neglecting skill development.
- **Lack of Work-Life Balance:**
    - Prioritizing work over personal time, always being on-call, neglecting personal interests.
- **Poor Time Management:**
    - Multitasking, not delegating, overcommitting, failing to prioritize tasks.
- **Ignoring Physical Environment:**
    - Working in a cluttered space, ignoring ergonomic needs, neglecting workspace comfort.

Burnout, decreased productivity, and a deterioration in the quality of work often follow, not to mention the personal toll on one's mental and physical health. Integrating self-care into the fabric of our professional lives becomes not just a private benefit but a strategic imperative.

This chapter explores self-care for all, aiming to shift perceptions and encourage a more balanced approach to work and well-being. Learn how to adopt a culture of comprehensive well-being within your organization. This discussion emphasizes the interconnectedness of individual well-being and collective success by exploring the versatile nature of self-care, from physical health to mental and emotional resilience. Here, self-care is not an afterthought but a vital component of leadership and followership that, when properly nurtured, becomes a powerful mechanism for achieving and sustaining organizational excellence.

Self-care, in principle, is universally important. However, in practice, it can vary significantly depending on the role you are playing at any given moment. For instance, a leader must practice a specific type of self-care that supports their responsibilities and the well-being of those they lead. This might include managing stress, setting a healthy example, and maintaining a balanced perspective.

On the other hand, a follower also needs to develop self-care practices, but these are oriented towards their unique position. Followers must be mindful of their boundaries, ensuring they do not overextend themselves while supporting the leader. This can involve setting clear limits on their time and energy and communicating their needs effectively.

Ultimately, both roles require an understanding of self-care tailored to their specific challenges and responsibilities. By recognizing these differences, individuals can cultivate a more effective and sustainable approach to maintaining their well-being.

This chapter invites leaders and followers to embrace well-being as a fundamental aspect of their roles. Through practical advice and real-world examples, you'll find the tools you need to integrate self-care into your daily routines. Self-care contributes to individuals' well-being and creates healthier, more vibrant organizations capable of thriving in today's dynamic landscape.

Understanding Self-Care

Self-care spans a broad spectrum of practices dedicated to nurturing one's physical, mental, and emotional health. Practicing self-care is about taking deliberate actions designed to replenish energy, mitigate stress, and bolster resilience. Although self-care is often misrepresented as selfish, in reality, self-care is a strategic act of self-preservation that strengthens your ability to lead with vigor or contribute meaningfully as a follower.

Incorporating self-care into your strategic planning is essential for executing your ideas without burning out. Self-care aligns seamlessly with other critical components of a successful strategy, such as financial vitality, a technology roadmap, and a product/service development plan. Most of us already understand that those elements are driving forces behind the progress of any organization, but fewer of us know why self-care is equally important.

Without a dedicated focus on self-care, the intricate pieces of the organizational puzzle can begin to shift out of place. As people burn out, lose focus, and become less productive, the overall harmony and efficiency of the organization can unravel, leading to misalignment and decreased effectiveness.

As leaders and teams push themselves beyond their limits in a misguided attempt to meet perceived organizational needs, the consequences are disastrous. A relentless drive toward results without concern for well-being can lead to end-of-year scrambles, widespread burnout, and a palpable sense of disengagement across the organization.

Self-care is the glue that holds these moving parts together, ensuring that the pursuit of organizational goals does not come at the expense of individual and team well-being. Incorporating self-care into your strategic plan requires recognizing that the organization's health is intrinsically linked to the health of its people. When leaders model and prioritize self-care, it communicates that they value sustainability over short-term gains, promoting an environment where people feel energized to do the same.

Thus, integrating self-care into our strategic approach is not optional—it's a critical factor that sustains the foundation of our organizational health. By weaving self-care into the fabric of our daily operations and culture, we safeguard our capacity to innovate, execute, and drive forward without sacrificing our most valuable asset: our people. This balanced approach ensures that as we pursue our organizational objectives, we have a capable, driven, resilient, and engaged workforce.

Self-Care in Practice

Leadership and followership are two sides of the same coin, and self-care is universally applicable, regardless of your role. Our roles change, requiring us to adapt our self-care strategies accordingly.

A followership role and the tasks that come with it are pivotal to any endeavor's success—but the focus on leadership can eclipse your well-being. Nonetheless, followers must prioritize self-care to sustain effectiveness, engagement, and job satisfaction. Burnout and exhaustion are not exclusive to leadership roles.

Leaders shoulder immense responsibilities, often at the expense of their well-being. Yet, overlooking self-care can cause burnout, impair performance, and damage team dynamics. Enlightened leaders view self-care as a critical duty—not an indulgence. They understand that self-nurturing enhances their capacity to inspire, motivate, and steer their teams toward excellence.

Self-care is a personal journey, not a one-size-fits-all solution. It's about discovering practices that resonate with you and enrich your well-being. Don't be too focus on what "others" say is self-care for you.

While self-care is often associated with those "fun" activities—which we will explore later in this chapter—this section focuses on self-care strategies that establish a consistent and sustainable routine. These practices may not offer the immediate enjoyment of those more recreational activities, but they provide a foundation for ongoing well-being and resilience.

Self-care isn't just about indulging in occasional treats or activities that bring temporary joy, such as spa days, vacations, or hobbies. These are certainly important and have their place, but for lasting benefits, it's crucial to incorporate self-care practices as a normal part of your core approach.

The strategies outlined below are designed to help you maintain a balanced lifestyle, reduce stress, and prevent burnout. Call them preventive self-care measures to support the maintenance of the day to day.

They involve setting boundaries, managing responsibilities, and seeking support—all of which contribute to a healthier, more manageable daily life. By integrating these practices into your routine, you can create a stable self-care regimen that supports your mental, emotional, and physical health consistently, not just in moments of relaxation.

Strategic Delegation

Strategic delegation helps you manage your workload more effectively, reducing stress and preventing burnout. By sharing responsibilities with your team based on their strengths, you can focus on higher-priority tasks and have more time for self-care.

Tactics:

- **Identify Strengths:** Assess the unique abilities and strengths of your team members to delegate tasks effectively. If John is great at vendor management and not so great excel, perhaps John can take on more vendor management and you shift the excel duties to another team members. (This is a balance, as cross training is also very important!)

- **Set Clear Expectations:** Clearly communicate the desired outcomes and deadlines for delegated tasks.

- **Provide Resources:** Ensure that team members have the necessary tools and support to complete their tasks.

- **Empower Team Members:** Trust your team to handle the responsibilities you delegate, embracing their growth and autonomy. An absolute destroyer of self-care is constant check-ins. Check-ins are fine, but being too frequent boarders micro-management, damaging both you and your team.

Mindfulness

Mindfulness encourages a present-focused approach, reducing stress and improving decision-making. Practicing mindfulness daily helps you stay calm and centered, enhancing your overall well-being and allowing you to lead more effectively.

Tactics:

- **Daily Mindfulness Practices:** Start your day with a meditation exercise to center yourself. Meditation does not always mean sitting cross legged on the floor with a candle focusing your mind and body. While this practice is helpful, and one I enjoy from time to time. Mindfulness can also be a morning cup of coffee sitting quietly reflecting. Or laying on the floor listening to music. Mindfulness is what you make it.

- **Active Listening:** Practice active listening during meetings and interactions to fully engage with your team.

    The active listening self-care strategy is one that I often get the most questions about. How can active listening be about self-care?

Active listening is often viewed purely as a communication skill, but it is also a powerful form of self-care. Engaging fully with others through active listening nurtures deeper and more meaningful relationships, providing emotional support and a sense of belonging that are crucial for mental and emotional health. This practice creates a calm and focused environment, reducing stress and anxiety by shifting your focus away from your own worries or thoughts in the moment. Active listening also enhances self-awareness and emotional intelligence, helping you manage your emotions more effectively. By demonstrating respect and validation for others, you build trust and empathy, strengthening your social network and boosting your self-esteem as others are more likely to reciprocate attentive listening when you are seeking their support.

Furthermore, active listening provides continuous learning opportunities, broadening your understanding and knowledge, which can be intellectually stimulating and fulfilling. It encourages a positive feedback loop in conversations, enhancing your mood and overall outlook by making interactions more productive and satisfying. Practical tips for practicing active listening include being present, showing engagement, reflecting and clarifying, empathizing, and responding thoughtfully. Incorporating active listening into your self-care routine not only improves your communication skills but also promotes a healthier, more optimistic mindset, creating a supportive and understanding environment for everyone involved.

- **Mindful Breaks:** Take short breaks throughout the day to clear your mind and reduce stress.
- **Reflective Practices:** Spend time reflecting on your decisions and actions to improve future outcomes.

Boundaries Between Work and Personal Life

Establishing clear boundaries between work and personal life ensures you have dedicated time for relaxation and personal interests. This separation is crucial for preventing burnout and maintaining a healthy balance, allowing you to recharge and engage fully in both areas.

Tactics:

- **Set Specific Work Hours:** Define and stick to specific work hours to prevent work from encroaching on personal time. Working hours are not always 8-5. If that is your organization working day, then be respectful of that. But if you are in a role of flexibility, creating set times is critical.

- **Schedule Personal Time:** Allocate time for hobbies, exercise, and relaxation to recharge outside of work. Seriously, book it on your calendar.

- **Digital Detox:** Implement periods of time where you disconnect from work-related emails and digital devices. – This is a powerful strategy, later on in this chapter we go into a bit more detail on digital detox and its overall impact on self-care.

- **Communicate Boundaries:** Clearly communicate your availability to colleagues and family to set expectations.

Seeking Support

Reaching out for support from mentors, peers, or professional counselors helps you navigate challenges more effectively. Building a support network provides emotional resilience and a sense of community, which are vital for maintaining mental health and well-being.

Tactics:

- **Build a Support Network:** Identify and cultivate relationships with mentors, peers, and trusted colleagues who can provide support. Support comes in all shapes and sizes. And sometimes, in our stressful working environment, some to listen while you vent it healthy. But be mindful of whom you vent to, it must be a well trusted college who understands your intention of needed to vent.

- **Utilize Employee Assistance Programs (EAP):** Take advantage of EAP services offered by your organization to speak with professional counselors.
    - I cannot emphasize enough the benefits of relying on my EAP for professional support. The EAP has been invaluable for managing stress, seeking guidance through challenging decisions, or navigating difficult conversations with employees, peers, or leadership. Seeking help, especially as a leader, is not optional—it's essential.
- **Regular Check-Ins:** Schedule regular meetings or check-ins with your support network to discuss challenges and seek advice. | Regular self-check ins are also very useful. Set 15–30-minute blocks of time for checking in on ourself to help set the intention that self-care is critical.
- **Professional Development:** Engage in professional development opportunities, such as coaching or counseling, to enhance your leadership skills and resilience.

By integrating these and other practices into your routine, you can cultivate a sustainable self-care strategy that enhances both your personal and professional life. Remember, the key to effective self-care is finding what works best for you and consistently making time for it. The above are simple ideas. What self-care ideas might work for you?

Many of us believe we can and should face the world alone—and there are times when we have to. However, it's worth considering how much better life could be with some assistance now and then. Self-reliance is powerful, yet the strength found in seeking support cannot be overstated. Knowing when to ask for help is a testament to the wisdom of effective leaders. Asking for help does not diminish your capabilities; it amplifies your ability to navigate complex situations more effectively. Authentic leadership is measured not by your ability to conquer alone but to succeed together.

Self-Care "My Meditation"

Self-care is not a one-size-fits-all practice, and it often needs to adapt to different roles and situations. I learned this firsthand when I had to shift from a leadership role to a followership role.

As I have mentioned before, when you hear the word "meditation," your first thoughts may immediately turn to sitting cross-legged on the floor, candles lit, and calm music in the background. I have engaged in this style of meditation when the need arises and continue to do so. However, as my self-care practices evolved, I began to recognize that meditation for me needed to be a unique experience, not a social or theatrical exercise that I felt obliged to perform. Not to cast any shade on traditional meditation practices, but I needed to create a meditation style that truly resonated with me. This is when I developed the "My Meditation" practice.

The "My Meditation" practice is a self-care philosophy that focuses on finding what meditation practices work best for you. Meditation is the deliberate practice of calming the mind and focusing one's attention to achieve a state of mental clarity, emotional tranquility, and heightened awareness. It is a disciplined act of introspection and contemplation, aimed at supporting inner peace and mental growth.

With that, "My Meditation" is all about discovering the meditation practice that suits you. Here are some of mine:

1. **Morning cup of coffee on the back porch**: Picture, if you will, a crisp morning with the soft light from the not-yet-fully-risen sun. The coo of a dove is the only sound breaking the silent tranquility. My cell phone is safely tucked away on the kitchen charging station. There are no distractions—just my coffee and those internal moments of "me time" to reflect and meditate.

2. **Building Lego with my son**: This meditation practice, while far from traditional, is a key part of my own "My Meditation." When engrossed in building Lego with my sweet William, I can recenter my focus and thoughts on what I feel is important to provide mental clarity for me: Family Time! I use this practice when I feel overwhelmed by life's demands. This meditation helps bring me back to why I am working so hard—my family—while also emphasizing the importance of self-care and spending time with loved ones.

    - Do I build Lego by myself sometimes? You bet I do. The meditation of a quick Lego build session allows my in-the-moment mind to focus on the building Lego tasks, while my subconscious mind meditates on whatever challenge I am facing. It is a real problem-solving regimen for me. And this practice doesn't need to be just Lego. It can be coloring a picture, completing a puzzle, or anything that allows your hands and conscious mind to engage in a familiar task requiring some creativity and thinking, while your subconscious mind meditates and brings clarity to deeper issues.

What could be some "My Mediation" practices that are unique to you? Think about it? Maybe it's something you wouldn't normally consider as mediation.

One area I ask that you please consider as not part of the "My Meditation" practice is screen time. In our digital age, it can be tempting to view activities such as scrolling through social media, binge-watching TV shows, or endlessly browsing the internet as forms of relaxation or even meditation. However, screen time often leads to mental clutter rather than clarity. The constant influx of information, notifications, and visual stimuli can overwhelm the mind, making it difficult to achieve the calm and focus that true meditation requires.

While there are many digital tools and apps designed to aid in meditation, it's crucial to differentiate between using these tools mindfully and allowing screen time to dominate your self-care routine. Engaging in activities that promote genuine mindfulness and introspection, free from the distractions of screens, is essential for cultivating a deeper sense of peace and mental clarity.

Consider instead practices that allow for direct, tactile engagement with the world around you, such as taking a walk in nature, engaging in creative hobbies, or spending quality time with loved ones. These activities can provide a more fulfilling and restorative meditation experience, aligning with the principles of "My Meditation."

By consciously limiting screen time and prioritizing activities that advance genuine mindfulness, you can create a more effective and personalized meditation practice that truly enhances your well-being. Which leads us into our next section on Digital Detox.

Digital Detox for Self-Care

In today's hyper-connected world, the idea of unplugging from our digital devices can seem almost radical. Yet, this practice, known as digital detox, is a vital self-care strategy. By taking a deliberate break from screens, we can significantly enhance our well-being and productivity. This article delves into the benefits of digital detox, offers some practical strategies for implementation, and provides tips for staying motivated.

We've all been there—doomscrolling, one of my favorite pastimes, is the easiest way to get lost in mindless distraction. How often have you looked at the clock, decided to scroll on your phone for five minutes, only to get trapped in doomscrolling and find that an hour has passed?

Or, boom—you wake up in the morning, grab your phone, and start reviewing emails, calendars, and other items that require your attention. Suddenly, you hear yourself saying, "I am already behind" before you've even gotten out of bed.

Both of these examples are detrimental to a self-care regimen.

That said, my personal journey has been marked by excessive screen time. In the past few months, I've even considered reinstalling an ancient device—a landline. My thought was to set boundaries: if it's an emergency, please call me. My landline will ring, and I will answer. Emails, texts, and other media might not receive an immediate response.

Instead of a landline, I came up with the idea of a "Cell Phone Lockbox"—a transparent lockbox where I can place my phone for digital detox breaks. I'll turn the ringer up and set exceptions for friends, family, and colleagues, informing them that during "family time" or "me time" (from hours X to Y), calling is the only way to reach me in an emergency. The clear lockbox provides a space to keep my phone while detoxing, and if it rings, I can see who's calling and choose whether to answer.

I had the pleasure of listening to Christine Cashen speak at a conference. Her humorous real-life examples of screen addiction served as a powerful reminder of the importance of a digital detox. It moved me to begin practical strategies for creating meaningful and intentional screen boundaries, both at home and in the workplace.

The Professional Perks of Unplugging

1. **Boosting Productivity:** Constant notifications and the ever-present lure of social media can wreak havoc on our ability to focus. Minimizing these distractions can lead to increased efficiency and improved quality of work.
2. **Igniting Creativity:** Freed from the relentless barrage of digital noise, our minds can wander and innovate. This mental space is crucial for creative thinking and problem-solving.
3. **Achieving Work-Life Balance:** Establishing boundaries between work and personal life is essential in preventing burnout. A digital detox can help draw these lines more clearly, promoting a healthier work routine.

Personal Gains from Digital Detox

1. **Enhancing Mental Health:** Excessive screen time is linked to anxiety, depression, and sleep disturbances. Taking a break from screens can uplift your mood, reduce stress, and improve overall mental health.
2. **Strengthening Relationships:** Being fully present in face-to-face interactions deepens our connections with loved ones. A digital detox encourages meaningful conversations and quality time with family and friends.
3. **Improving Physical Health:** Reducing screen time can alleviate physical issues like eye strain, headaches, and neck pain. It also encourages more physical activity, which is beneficial for overall health.

Practical Strategies for a Successful Digital Detox

1. **Set Clear Goals:** Define what you hope to achieve with your digital detox, whether it's reducing stress, improving focus, or spending more time with family. Clear goals will help you stay motivated.

2. **Create Tech-Free Zones:** Establish areas in your home where digital devices are not allowed, such as the dining room, bedroom, children's playroom, kitchen, or wherever moves you. These spaces become sanctuaries free from digital distractions.
3. **Schedule Digital Downtime:** Plan specific times each day or week to unplug, such as during meals, an hour before bedtime, or (if you are extra brave) the entire weekend.
4. **Use Digital Detox Apps:** Various apps can help monitor and limit your screen time, offering insights into your digital habits and assisting in setting boundaries.
5. **Engage in Offline Activities:** Fill your time with activities that don't involve screens. Reading a book, going for a walk, practicing a hobby, or spending time with friends and family are fulfilling alternatives.
6. **Gradual Reduction:** If the idea of a complete detox seems daunting, start by gradually reducing your screen time. Cut down by 30 minutes each day until you reach a comfortable balance.

Navigating the Challenges and Staying Motivated

1. **Acknowledge the Challenge:** Adjusting to less screen time may be difficult initially. You might feel restless or experience FOMO (fear of missing out). These feelings are normal and will diminish over time.
2. **Celebrate Small Wins:** Recognize and celebrate your progress, no matter how small. Each step towards reducing screen time is a victory.
3. **Stay Accountable:** Share your digital detox goals with friends or family who can support and hold you accountable.
4. **Reflect on the Benefits:** Keep a journal to note the positive changes you experience during your detox. Reflecting on improved mood, better sleep, and enhanced relationships can reinforce your commitment.

5. **Be Flexible:** It's okay to adjust your detox plan as needed. Life is unpredictable, and sometimes you may need to be flexible with your goals. The key is to maintain a balanced approach.

A digital detox is more than just a temporary break from technology; it's a profound act of self-care that can significantly enhance both your professional and personal life. By intentionally stepping back from screens, you can reclaim your time, boost your well-being, and rediscover the joys of offline living. Embrace the digital detox journey—it's an investment in yourself that pays dividends in countless ways.

Expanding on the Concept of Fun Self-Care

Self-care isn't just about relaxation—it's about recharging, reconnecting with your interests, and encouraging a sense of joy and fulfillment. Here's a deeper look into several suggested "fun" self-care activities and their benefits:

- **Picnics in the Park:** A simple yet profoundly relaxing activity, picnics offer a chance to enjoy nature, indulge in your favorite foods, and perhaps share quality time with loved ones. A picnic combines the benefits of fresh air, a change of scenery, and the pleasure of culinary delights, providing a perfect escape from the daily grind.

- **Visiting the Spa:** Even a brief visit to a spa can significantly lift your spirits. Whether it's a massage, a facial, or a soak in a thermal bath, spa treatments can reduce stress, soothe your body, and promote a sense of well-being, reminding you of the importance of nurturing yourself.

- **Cooking Parties:** Hosting a cooking party brings together the joy of preparing and sharing a meal with friends or family. Cooking together fosters community and connection and allows for creative expression through culinary arts, turning meal preparation into a festive, enriching experience.

- **Outdoor Adventures:** Hiking, biking, kayaking, camping, and other outdoor adventures invigorate the spirit and challenge the body. Engaging with the natural world provides a unique sense of freedom and perspective, reminding us of the beauty of the world beyond our immediate concerns.

- **Game Nights:** Organizing a game night is a fantastic way to unwind and engage in playful competition with friends or family. Board games, card games, and video games can stimulate the mind, encourage laughter and camaraderie, and create lasting memories.

- **Creative Crafting:** Diving into a crafting project—painting, Lego, pottery, or any other creative art—offers a meditative escape. Crafting can boost your creativity, provide a sense of accomplishment, and provide a tangible reminder of the time spent caring for yourself.

- **Karaoke Sessions:** Singing your heart out during a karaoke session can be incredibly liberating. Whether you're a seasoned vocalist or in it for laughs, karaoke is a great way to express yourself, relieve stress, and enjoy music in a new, interactive way.

- **Outdoor Movie Nights:** Setting up an outdoor movie night in your backyard or a community space combines the magic of cinema with the beauty of the outdoors. Watching a movie outside is a unique way to immerse yourself in storytelling under the stars, offering a novel alternative to the traditional movie-going experience.

- **Photography Walks:** Taking a camera (use a real camera, not your cell phone!) and embarking on a photography walk encourages mindfulness as you search for beauty in your surroundings. Photography walks can enhance your observational skills, raise creativity, and provide a rewarding way to explore new or familiar environments through a different lens.

- **Dance Parties:** Hosting a dance party, even if it's just in your living room with a few close friends or by yourself, is a joyous way to celebrate life, release endorphins, and enjoy the moment. Dancing can lift your mood, boost your energy level, and allow for uninhibited self-expression.

Each activity underscores the importance of taking time for yourself, not as a luxury but as a critical component of a balanced and fulfilling life. By regularly incorporating such experiences into our routines, we can maintain a better sense of well-being, creativity, and joy.

What's Not Self-Care

Self-care has become a buzzword in recent years, often focusing on spa days, shopping sprees, and indulgences. All of these can be aspects of self-care, but it's crucial to identify what self-care isn't to fully grasp its essence and impact on our well-being.

- **Self-Care Isn't Just Indulgence:** First and foremost, self-care isn't merely about indulging in material pleasures, pampering, or luxuries. Treating yourself to a nice meal or a new outfit can be part of self-care; these actions alone do not encompass the depth and breadth of genuine self-care practices. Proper self-care involves activities supporting your mental, physical, and emotional health, ensuring long-term well-being rather than a temporary feel-good factor.
- **Self-Care Isn't Avoidance:** Self-care isn't about avoiding or escaping problems. Using self-care as a means to

sidestep dealing with challenging issues, responsibilities, or emotions can lead to a cycle of avoidance that ultimately compounds stress. Authentic self-care confronts difficulties head-on, equipping you with the resilience you need to manage life's inevitable ups and downs.

- **Self-Care Isn't Selfishness:** Self-care is often mistakenly conflated with selfishness. Far from being selfish, genuinely prioritizing your well-being is essential for maintaining your health and happiness, enabling you to be more present and supportive of others. Self-care is a necessary practice for sustaining your ability to empathize, not a selfish withdrawal from caring about those around you.

- **Self-Care Isn't One-Size-Fits-All:** Self-care is highly individualized. What works for one person might not work for another. There is no one-size-fits-all solution to stress, fatigue, or other issues. Effective self-care requires introspection and understanding what nourishes your body and soul, whether it's quiet time alone, engaging in physical activity, pursuing creative hobbies, or seeking social connections.

- **Self-Care Isn't Just for Times of Crisis:** Lastly, self-care shouldn't be reserved for moments of crisis or when you're at your breaking point. It's a continuous, proactive practice that should be integrated into your daily routine. Waiting until you are overwhelmed neglects the preventive aspect of self-care, which should consistently maintain your well-being.

Self-care is a multifaceted practice that goes beyond superficial treatments to address your core mental, physical, and emotional health needs. Engaging in self-care involves taking intentional actions to improve your quality of life, not seeking temporary pleasures or escapism. By understanding what self-care is not, we can better appreciate its actual value and incorporate it meaningfully into our lives.

Generating a Culture of Self-Care

Creating and nurturing a culture of self-care within an organization is a collaborative endeavor requiring active participation and dedication from leaders and followers. Leaders need to lead by example, demonstrating a steadfast commitment to self-care in their practices and the policies and environments they cultivate. A leadership approach that includes self-care sets a powerful precedent, promoting a workplace atmosphere that values well-being.

Leaders must integrate self-care into the fabric of organizational life, making it clear that taking care of oneself is not merely encouraged but is integral to professional success and personal growth. Integrating self-care can involve implementing flexible work arrangements, encouraging regular breaks, providing resources for mental and physical health, and creating spaces for relaxation within the workplace.

If you have the capacity to influence or enact change, consider actively leveraging your systems to promote well-being. Implement standards that require generating reports on employees' time off. Reviewing these reports lets you identify if an employee is forgoing necessary self-care breaks for extended periods and allows you to intervene before an employee burns out.

When you're exploring ways to enhance self-care, engagement, and employee benefits, recognize that two weeks of paid time off may not suffice. Two weeks is a slim percentage of the entire year. This minimal allocation of time off forces employees to choose between saving days for illness or sparingly using them for much-needed vacations, potentially leading to taking unpaid leave or working while sick. The latter scenario, where an employee works through illness, starkly contradicts self-care principles. Employees who come to work while sick indicate a failure of leadership.

As a leader, I urge you to consider increasing the minimum paid time off to three weeks for every employee, ensuring everyone has ample opportunity for self-care. This additional week represents a minor increase—a mere two percent (1.92% based on 260 days)—yet it could significantly enhance employees' well-being and work-life balance. Increasing paid time off is a necessary step toward a healthier, more productive workplace environment.

Instilling company policies on self-care, such as providing ample sick leave and promoting a culture of wellness, is essential for maintaining a healthy workforce. However, leaders must take this a step further by actively supporting their employees' recovery when they are ill. This means not only implementing these policies but also encouraging and facilitating their use.

Leaders can:

- **Encourage Sick Leave:** Clearly communicate to employees that they should take their sick leave when needed. Emphasize that their health is a priority, and that rest is essential for recovery.

- **Model Healthy Behavior:** When leaders take time off to recover from illness, it sets a positive example. It shows employees that it's acceptable and encourages them to prioritize their health.

- **Provide Flexible Options:** Offer flexible work arrangements, such as remote work or adjusted hours, to accommodate employees who are recovering but may still need to manage some work tasks.

- **Monitor Workload:** Ensure that sick employees are not overburdened with work. Reassign tasks or adjust deadlines as needed to reduce stress and facilitate recovery.

- **Communicate Supportively:** Maintain open and supportive communication. Regularly check in on the employee's well-being without pressuring them to return to work before they are ready.

- **Access to Resources:** Inform employees about available health resources offered by your organization, such as virtual doctor consultations, employee assistance programs (EAP), and other health services.

By actively promoting rest and recovery, leaders can help employees return to work healthier and more productive, while also developing a supportive and caring workplace culture.

However, each situation is unique and must be evaluated individually. Sometimes, allowing the employee to work remotely, have flexible hours, or engage in low-level activities is appropriate. Other times, it's necessary to issue a direct order for them not to work. While I usually avoid giving direct orders, when an employee's well-being is at risk, my inner five-star general emerges, and direct orders are given. In such cases, I would even advocate for our technology department to intervene by temporarily locking the employee's account to enforce a period of rest.

Followers also play a crucial role in reinforcing a culture of self-care. By actively taking responsibility for their well-being, they enhance their resilience and contribute to a more supportive, understanding, and empathetic work environment. Followers can champion self-care by engaging in open conversations about well-being, participating in and advocating for wellness initiatives, and supporting their peers in self-care efforts.

The mutual commitment to self-care by leaders and followers serves as a foundation for building resilience across all levels of the organization. Resilience becomes a key driver of productivity, as employees who feel supported are more likely to be engaged, motivated, and committed to their work. Furthermore, a culture that prioritizes well-being helps to mitigate burnout, reduce absenteeism, and advance a more positive workplace atmosphere.

Beyond enhancing individual productivity and fulfillment, the collective embrace of self-care contributes to the vitality of the organization as a whole. A workplace that values self-care is adaptable, vibrant, and sustainable. Such workplaces can attract and retain top talent, encourage innovation, and enhance the reputation for being a caring and responsible employer. Ultimately, the commitment to well-being doesn't just elevate personal fulfillment and success; it becomes a cornerstone of the organization's identity, reflecting a profound understanding that the health of the organization is inextricably linked to the well-being of its people.

Chapter 6: Combating Burnout

Burnout is the modern manifestation of overwork. Fifty years ago, people started using the term "burnout" in the context we understand it today, thanks to the work of psychologist Herbert Freudenberger (Samra, Rajvinder. "Brief History of Burnout." BMJ, vol. 363, 2018). He is credited with bringing the term into the mainstream by describing burnout as a state of mental and physical exhaustion caused by one's professional life. Before the term "burnout" became widely recognized, related symptoms might have been described using terms like "exhaustion," "nervous breakdown," or "stress reaction." Earlier terms captured the essence of what we now refer to as burnout but lacked a specific focus on workplace-related stressors and a comprehensive understanding of its impact on mental health.

Burnout is, in essence, when the demands of work, personal aspirations, and societal expectations collide; the phenomenon has emerged as a formidable challenge. Burnout is a state of emotional, physical, and mental exhaustion caused by prolonged stress that diminishes an individual's well-being and capacity to thrive professionally and personally.

Burnout can affect anyone, regardless of their profession. It often stems from the nature of the work itself. Working continuously without breaks is exhausting. I know from experience; on days when I jump from virtual meeting to virtual meeting, I feel completely burned out. Trying to squeeze in a few minutes to clean up emails or complete action items between 5 p.m. and 6 p.m. is where I get stuck, allowing burnout to take control. If only I could step away, recognize the signs of burnout, and schedule my meetings more effectively, blocking off time to complete emails and tasks. But office work aside, burnout can impact any profession—medical, construction, teaching, you name it. We all experience burnout.

This chapter explores burnout, including its signs, consequences, and, most importantly, strategies to combat it, paving the way for sustainable success.

Understanding Burnout

Burnout manifests through a constellation of symptoms that, when left unchecked, can profoundly affect an individual's emotional, physical, and mental well-being. Leaders and individuals should be on the lookout for three main dimensions that indicate the presence of burnout: overwhelming exhaustion, cynicism about and detachment from work, and an overarching sense of ineffectiveness.

- **Emotional and Physical Exhaustion:** Constant fatigue, insomnia, and a perpetual state of dread regarding the day ahead.

- **Cynicism and Detachment:** A growing sense of disillusionment with one's work or personal life, leading to isolation.
- **Ineffectiveness:** The feeling that one's efforts are meaningless, leading to decreased productivity and satisfaction.

Overwhelming exhaustion extends beyond mere tiredness. Burnout-level exhaustion encapsulates a profound depletion of emotional and physical energy. Individuals who have reached this level of fatigue feel drained of the capability to face daily tasks. This exhaustion often results in a diminished interest in work, where tasks once approached with enthusiasm now invoke indifference.

Feelings of cynicism and detachment from the job constitute the second dimension of burnout. This symptom reflects a growing sense of disconnection from one's work and colleagues. What starts as a protective measure to emotionally distance oneself from stressors gradually morphs into a pervasive sense of disillusionment, often spilling over into interactions outside the workplace.

The third hallmark of burnout is a pervasive sense of ineffectiveness and lack of accomplishment. Individuals may begin to doubt their skills and contributions, feeling that no matter how much effort they expend, their work does not yield meaningful outcomes. This erosion of self-efficacy and professional satisfaction can lead to a cycle of decreased productivity and increased self-criticism.

Burnout doesn't occur overnight; it's the culmination of prolonged exposure to stress and imbalance in various aspects of life, including work demands, personal challenges, and lifestyle factors. The gradual onset of burnout underscores the importance of early detection and intervention. Identifying the early signs of burnout—such as persistent fatigue, irritability, changes in sleep patterns, anxiety, and a decrease in job performance—is the first step toward mitigating its impact.

Understanding these dimensions and their manifestations allows for a more nuanced approach to identifying and combating burnout. Strategies to counteract burnout involve a comprehensive approach that includes setting clear work-life boundaries, adopting a supportive work environment, engaging in regular self-care practices, and seeking support. Individuals and organizations that acknowledge the multifaceted nature of burnout can take proactive steps to cultivate a healthier, more balanced approach to work and life.

Consequences of Ignoring Burnout

In my career as a leader in the credit union industry, I had the privilege of working with a truly brilliant individual, Emily.

Her intellect, communication skills, and consistent delivery of exceptional results set her apart. However, she was clearly grappling with severe burnout—a condition she managed to mask while continuing to meet and exceed her obligations. The burnout was taking a toll on her in ways she couldn't fully realize. It's often said that one cannot see the whole picture when they are within the frame, and this was precisely her situation. And because she was an extremely high performer, spotting the signs of burnout was very difficult.

Burnout in high performers can be particularly challenging to identify because these individuals often push themselves to maintain high standards despite increasing stress and exhaustion. Not allowing their burnout symptoms to show to their leadership, peers, friends, or even their families.

Here are some key signs to look out for:

Decreased Performance

- **Decline in Productivity**: Tasks take longer to complete, and the quality of work may suffer.
- **Missed Deadlines**: Frequent delays or last-minute rushes to meet deadlines.

Emotional Exhaustion

- **Chronic Fatigue**: Persistent tiredness that doesn't improve with rest.
- **Irritability and Mood Swings**: Increased frustration, impatience, or emotional outbursts.

Detachment and Cynicism

- **Withdrawal from Work**: Reduced enthusiasm and engagement in tasks they once enjoyed.
- **Negative Attitude**: A more cynical or pessimistic outlook towards their job or colleagues.

Physical Symptoms

- **Frequent Illness**: Increased susceptibility to colds or other illnesses.
- **Physical Aches**: Unexplained headaches, muscle pain, or other physical complaints.

Cognitive Difficulties

- **Difficulty Concentrating**: Trouble focusing on tasks or making decisions.
- **Memory Problems**: Forgetfulness or difficulty recalling information.

Behavioral Changes

- **Increased Absenteeism**: Taking more sick days or arriving late/leaving early more frequently.
- **Social Withdrawal**: Avoiding social interactions with colleagues or isolating themselves.

Lack of Personal Satisfaction

- **Loss of Motivation**: Decreased enthusiasm or passion for work.
- **Feeling of Ineffectiveness**: A sense that their efforts are not making a difference.

Neglecting Personal Needs

- **Poor Self-Care**: Skipping meals, neglecting exercise, or not getting enough sleep.
- **Work-Life Imbalance**: Spending excessive hours at work and neglecting personal life.

Recognizing these signs early can help address burnout before it leads to more severe consequences. It's crucial for leaders to create an environment that supports the well-being of their team members and encourages open communication about stress and workload management

Let's revisit Emily, who, despite displaying signs of burnout, continued to exemplify excellence in her work. Her communication skills were exceptional, effortlessly bridging gaps and raising understanding among team members. Emily had an uncanny ability to address immediate needs while strategically planning for the future, ensuring long-term success while meeting short-term objectives. In her unofficial yet indispensable roles in business intelligence, project management, technology, and as the go-to person for many of the most complex tasks, she consistently outperformed her peers and even her seniors. Despite her high performance, the signs of burnout were subtle but present, making it crucial for me, as her leader, to recognize and address them to maintain her well-being and continued success.

When I first met Emily, she was working on a different team, but I was fully aware of her skill set and her performance accomplishments. When an opportunity arose for her to join my team, I eagerly seized it, fully aware that an initial part of my role would involve assisting her in navigating through her long-term burnout. I believed that once she overcame this hurdle and was equipped with the tools to manage burnout and prevent its long-term recurrence, she would thrive, especially when surrounded by the support she previously lacked. While recovery from extreme burnout can take months to years, I knew that Emily would emerge on the other side as a formidable leader capable of not only guiding others but also pushing results and deliverables to new heights. In the role I envisioned for her, we would work together to ensure she receives value from her need to exemplify excellence and delivery results, while we addressed her burnout and laying the groundwork for her future progression.

Some leaders assume that as long as an employee is performing well, stress and burnout are issues the employee needs to handle on their own time. Nothing could be further from the truth. This "let them handle it on their own" approach can be costly, leading to high turnover, disengagement, and the loss of top talent.

Recognizing these potential costs of not addressing burnout, my leadership team and I decided to take proactive steps. We restructured Emily's workload to ensure it was more manageable, provided her with adequate rest and recovery, and made resources for stress management readily available. Additionally, we instituted regular one-on-one meetings to discuss her progress and any ongoing challenges, offering a safe space for her to voice her concerns and needs. We also encouraged a culture of open communication and support within the team, emphasizing the importance of mental health and work-life balance.

Furthermore, we offered Emily opportunities for professional development and growth that aligned with her passions and strengths, helping to rekindle her enthusiasm and drive. We also implemented flexible work arrangements, allowing her to have better control over her schedule and workload. By addressing the root causes of her burnout and providing comprehensive support, we aimed to not only help Emily recover but also to set a precedent for how to effectively manage and prevent burnout within our organization.

And while all of the above was helpful in supporting Emily, the biggest and most important aspect of helping an individual recover from burnout is this: having a transparent conversation with them. Discuss with them that they are exceptional but are showing signs of burnout. This can be difficult for any individual, especially high performers, to hear. They may deny the burnout, not wanting to appear unable to complete tasks or maintain their workload. They might challenge you, asking if they have missed something or made a mistake.

It is critical for you as the leader to assure them that this is not a performance issue or concern whatsoever. You must show compassion and understanding. Be transparent with them, affirming that they are extremely high performers but are exhibiting signs of burnout. Support them by saying, "We will work through this together."

Above all, you must communicate to them that during the burnout recovery process, they will not be overlooked for opportunities, raises, or seen as underperforming in any way. Assure them that you recognize their immense value and that you, as their leader, are protecting your most valuable asset: your people! This protection includes having the difficult discussion that you are committed to working through their burnout together.

This approach with Emily produced remarkable results. She regained her energy, enthusiasm, and creativity. Her productivity soared to new heights, and she once again became the linchpin of the team, driving projects to successful completion with renewed vigor.

This example clearly demonstrates the importance of addressing burnout. Ignoring it can lead to a decline in performance and well-being, while proactive measures can enhance both employee satisfaction and productivity. Emily's story underscores that supporting high performers in managing stress is not just beneficial but essential for sustaining long-term success.

As a leader, one of your highest priorities must be protecting your high performers, even from themselves. They will always be your most valuable asset. Protect them, care for them, and support them. Ensure you are leading them through burnout directly, not just outlining the tools they need to overcome it. Effective followership plays a significant role in combating burnout. For example, putting everything on your high performer will create burnout. If they are the ace, then you need to shift gears and follow them by taking on some of the less desirable tasks, allowing them to focus on what makes them a superstar. Too often, I see high performers taking on more and more from their leaders out of a misguided sense of loyalty: "I must take everything I can from my leader; this is why they are in that role." While this can sometimes be true, it's far more effective when the leader assumes this position. Why? Because the leader has the authority to say "no" and take on these bottom-of-the-barrel tasks, allowing the high performer to focus on the complex items for which they were hired.

This approach to leadership and followership is about seeing beyond an individual's immediate contributions and investing in their long-term growth. Helping someone heal and harness their full potential aids them personally and cultivates a more dynamic, resilient team.

Here are some strategies for combating burnout:

Strategies to Combat Burnout

Self-Reflection and Acknowledgment The journey to overcoming burnout begins with self-reflection. Acknowledging that you're experiencing burnout is not a sign of weakness but the first step in reclaiming your well-being and zest for life.

Burnout Recognition Checklist:

Place a check mark next to each one that may apply to you.

Physical Symptoms

- **Chronic Fatigue**: Do you feel tired all the time, even after a good night's sleep?
- **Insomnia**: Are you having difficulty falling or staying asleep, despite feeling exhausted?
- **Frequent Illnesses**: Have you noticed an increased susceptibility to colds, flu, or other illnesses?
- **Headaches and Muscle Pain**: Do you frequently experience tension headaches or muscle aches?
- **Changes in Appetite or Sleep Habits**: Have you observed a noticeable increase or decrease in your appetite or sleep patterns?

Emotional Symptoms

- **Feelings of Overwhelm**: Do you constantly feel overwhelmed by work or personal responsibilities?
- **Emotional Numbness**: Are you feeling detached or indifferent towards work, colleagues, or daily activities?
- **Increased Irritability**: Do you find yourself becoming easily frustrated or angry, often over minor issues?

- **Lack of Motivation**: Is it difficult for you to start or complete tasks that were once enjoyable or manageable?
- **Sense of Failure or Self-Doubt**: Do you have persistent feelings of inadequacy or frequently question your competence?

Mental Symptoms

- **Reduced Concentration**: Are you having difficulty focusing on tasks or maintaining attention for long periods?
- **Memory Problems**: Do you forget important tasks, deadlines, or meetings?
- **Decreased Productivity**: Have you noticed a decline in your work output or quality?
- **Indecisiveness**: Are you struggling to make decisions or second-guessing your choices frequently?
- **Negative Outlook**: Do you have a pervasive sense of pessimism or feel hopeless about the future?

Behavioral Symptoms

- **Withdrawing from Responsibilities**: Are you avoiding work or personal responsibilities and procrastinating frequently?
- **Isolating from Others**: Do you find yourself pulling away from social interactions or feeling disconnected from colleagues and loved ones?
- **Using Substances to Cope**: Have you increased your reliance on alcohol, drugs, or food to manage stress?
- **Neglecting Self-Care**: Are you ignoring personal hygiene, exercise, or other self-care routines?

- **Increased Absenteeism**: Are you taking more sick days or time off than usual?

Job-Related Symptoms

- **Lack of Accomplishment**: Do you feel unappreciated or that your work is not meaningful?
- **Detachment from Work**: Have you developed a cynical attitude towards your job or colleagues?
- **Work-Life Imbalance**: Are you struggling to balance your professional and personal life, often taking work home?
- **Avoiding Work-Related Activities**: Do you feel reluctant to engage in work meetings, projects, or initiatives?
- **Decrease in Job Satisfaction**: Have you noticed an overall decline in your job satisfaction or interest in professional growth?

Use this checklist to regularly assess your well-being and recognize early signs of burnout. Checking multiple boxes in each category may indicate that you're experiencing burnout.

Now for the tough ask. Have the burnout discussion with your leadership. It will be difficult; it will be scary. But if they are the right leaders, they will recognize and support you without it leading to missed opportunities. If your current leader isn't the right person to discuss your concerns openly and effectively, without hindering your progress, and who won't listen and take action, then it's time to seek out someone in your organization who will. It's only fair to give your leader a chance to improve, but it's crucial for both your well-being and the health of your organization to find a leader who is willing to listen, understand, and provide the necessary support and guidance.

Should you find that no such leaders exist within your organization, it might be time to consider exploring other opportunities.

Remember, work will always be there, but there is no amount of money that can buy back your youth. Don't let long-term burnout rob you of the precious time you have. While occasional feelings of burnout are normal, enduring long-term burnout is dangerous and can have serious repercussions on your health and happiness.

As the follower, you have a responsibility to talk to your leader about possible burnout. As a leader, you must listen with compassion and reassurance.

Additional Strategies for Burnout can include:

Seek Support: Burnout can cloud your judgment, making it difficult to see a way out. Seeking support from friends, family, or professionals can provide new perspectives.

Set Boundaries: Setting clear boundaries is vital in an era where work and personal life often blend. This includes setting designated work hours, scheduling regular breaks, and taking time off. Learning to say no is a powerful tool in maintaining these boundaries.

Prioritize Self-Care: Invest in activities that replenish your energy and bring you joy. Whether it's exercise, hobbies, meditation, or quiet time alone, prioritize activities that nurture your mental and physical health.

Reevaluate, Realign, and Develop Resilience: Take time to reassess your goals, values, and what truly matters. This reevaluation might mean realigning your career path, redefining success, or rediscovering your sidelined passions. Building resilience involves cultivating a positive mindset, practicing gratitude, and focusing on solutions rather than problems. Resilience doesn't eliminate stress or erase life's difficulties, but it can empower you to navigate challenges more easily.

Embrace Mindfulness and Meditation: Mindfulness and meditation ("*My Meditation" from chapter 5*) can significantly reduce stress levels and enhance overall well-being. Mindfulness practices like meditation, breathing exercises, yoga, tai-chi, and similar practices help anchor you in the present moment, offering a reprieve from the constant churn of worries.

Implement Healthy Work Habits: Building healthy work habits includes taking regular breaks, practicing time management, and ensuring a positive work environment. Small changes in your daily work habits can significantly improve how you feel about your job and yourself.

Cultivate a Supportive Network: Build relationships with people who understand what you're going through and can provide encouragement and support. A strong support network can be a lifeline during tough times.

Recognizing Burnout in Leadership Roles

As a leader, the responsibility of recognizing burnout extends beyond self-awareness. The well-being of your team is also critical. If you're in a leadership role, you must be vigilant for signs of burnout in your followers. Be on the lookout for signs such as decreased productivity, increased absenteeism, or a noticeable drop in enthusiasm and creativity. Other indicators include a change in behavior patterns—irritability, withdrawal, or a decline in work quality. Indications of burnout can be subtle and require you to be attuned to your team's dynamics and individual behaviors.

Leaders are pivotal in creating an environment that recognizes and actively combats burnout. Here are strategies to support your team:

- **Open Lines of Communication** Foster an environment that encourages open, honest communication. Regular check-ins and one-on-one meetings can provide a safe space for followers to express concerns, challenges, or feelings of overwhelm without fear of judgment or reprisal. Ask, "How are you doing?" Don't just focus on how projects are going or what issue your team members are addressing, but how they are doing amid all of their priorities.

- **Lead by Example** Model healthy work-life balance practices. Show your team that they can take breaks, prioritize their well-being, and set boundaries. Your behavior sets the tone for your team's work culture. Laugh, joke, and bond with everyone within your team. Leading by example is a great way to show your team how to communicate.

- **Provide Resources and Support** Equip your team with resources to manage stress and prevent burnout. Helpful resources include access to mental health days, wellness programs, and professional development opportunities focused on building resilience and managing stress. If your organization has an Employee Assistance Program (EAP), promote this service and its use. If you want assistance sharing resources with your team, reach out to Human Resources for support.

- **Empower and Delegate** Empower your followers by entrusting them with meaningful responsibilities aligned with their strengths and interests. Delegation alleviates your workload and enhances a follower's sense of engagement. Delegation immediately followed by constant checks is not delegation; that is micromanaging, one of the leading causes of burnout.

- **Recognize and Reward Efforts** Acknowledge your team's hard work and achievements. Recognition is a powerful motivator and can counteract feelings of ineffectiveness, a hallmark of burnout. Small things make the most significant difference. As leaders, we may not always be able to pay employees what we want or provide them with the time off they deserve. However, personal handwritten messages and other small tokens are meaningful, showing respect and gratitude.

- **Encourage Team Building and Social Support** Promote a team culture that values support and collaboration. Team-building activities and informal social gatherings can strengthen bonds among team members, providing an additional layer of emotional support.

- **Advocate for Work-Life Harmony** Encourage your followers to find a balance between their work life and personal life. Respect their time off and support flexible work arrangements where possible.

As leaders, recognizing and addressing burnout in ourselves and our followers is crucial for sustaining a healthy, productive work environment. You can mitigate the effects of burnout by taking proactive steps to support and empower your team and develop a culture of well-being and resilience.

Moving Forward

Combating burnout is not a one-time task but an ongoing process of self-care, boundary-setting, and personal growth. Preventing burnout is about making daily conscious choices that contribute to your well-being and align with your values. As you implement these strategies, remember that seeking a balanced and fulfilling life is a journey—there will be ups and downs. Embrace each step with kindness for yourself and a commitment to navigating toward a brighter, more balanced future.

Dealing with burnout involves continual learning and self-compassion. If you struggle to maintain strategies against burnout or notice a regression into behaviors that exacerbate stress and exhaustion, practicing forgiveness toward yourself is crucial.

Recognizing these patterns is a significant step forward. Perfection isn't the goal—your earnest efforts to address burnout are valuable in their own right. Acknowledging that you're facing difficulties and making attempts to adjust and cope is a testament to your resilience.

Progress is often non-linear, and every effort you make contributes to your overall well-being and capacity to manage stress. Learn from each experience, understanding that with time and persistence, you'll find the best strategies. Burnout is developed over time; reversing burnout is a marathon, not a sprint (unless you win the lottery.) In that case, if you could please arrange for a sum of funds to be delivered, that would allow an individual like me to retire early. I would appreciate any help you can provide!).

Chapter 7: Caring Not to Care

Regardless of your role, one of the most profound lessons you can learn is mastering the art of "Caring Not to Care." This principle is not about indifference or disengagement but about cultivating a balanced perspective that allows leaders and independent contributors to invest their energies wisely, distinguishing between what truly matters and what does not.

How many of us find ourselves lying awake at night, our minds tirelessly replaying words and actions that, in all likelihood, others have long forgotten? Letting our imagination take the reins can send us spiraling into a whirlwind of self-defeating narratives. The tendency to overthink matters of fleeting importance traps us in a web of tension, stress, and mental fog.

We fabricate scenarios and dwell on interactions that hold little to no consequence in the grand scheme of things, yet they disrupt our peace and clarity. Magnifying trivialities robs us of tranquility and impedes our capacity to focus on what genuinely deserves our attention.

The Paradox of Care

At first glance, the notion of caring not to care seems contradictory. This concept is rooted in selective engagement—caring deeply about the mission, values, goals, and people that define our personal and professional lives while simultaneously releasing our grip on factors outside our control. Caring not to care involves letting go of the insignificant details that consume disproportionate amounts of our attention.

Consider the undue attention we often give to our appearance during virtual meetings. How often do you catch yourself checking your image on the screen? You might scrutinize your hair, your smile, or the way you react to conversations. Now think back to your last virtual meeting. Can you honestly recall whether any of the other participants had a bad hair day?

This underscores the importance of focusing on what truly matters and letting go of trivial concerns.

Discerning What Matters

The starting point in caring not to care is discernment. Discernment is the ability to perceive and understand what truly warrants focus by seeing beyond superficial distractions. It involves a deep awareness of core values and goals, enabling individuals to prioritize effectively and make decisions that align with their fundamental principles and long-term objectives. In leadership, discernment is crucial for navigating complex challenges and avoiding burnout by concentrating on what genuinely matters and is within one's control.

Developing discernment involves cultivating the ability to see beyond the surface level and identify what truly warrants our focus. This process is not just about prioritizing tasks but about aligning with a deeper understanding of what fundamentally drives us.

Leadership, in particular, demands a keen sense of discernment; the weight of your decisions, challenges, and expectations can easily lead to burnout without it. Effective leaders must navigate a landscape cluttered with distractions, demands, and noise, requiring a clear vision of what is truly important.

Start practicing discernment by engaging in the following activities:

- **Identify Core Values and Goals**: Clarify what is most important to you and your organization. Core values and goals should be the lighthouses guiding your decision-making process. These are not just abstract concepts but the bedrock of your purpose and direction. Reflect deeply on what you and your team stand for, and let these principles illuminate your path forward.

- **Assess Influence and Control**: When you find yourself starting to overthink, ask yourself, "Do I have control over this? Can I influence the outcome?" If the answer is no, the issue may be a candidate for not caring. Don't spend your time worrying over the issue; instead, focus on the resolution, or if no resolution is required, concentrate on what's more in alignment with your values, goals, and locus of control. This practice not only conserves your energy but also sharpens your focus on what truly matters, fostering a more purposeful and resilient approach to leadership.

By honing discernment, we learn to sift through the noise and zero in on what genuinely requires our attention. This refined focus empowers us to lead with clarity, purpose, and a profound sense of alignment with our core values.

Embracing Emotional Agility

Emotional agility is the capacity to navigate life's twists and turns with self-acceptance, clarity, and an open mind. When you're emotionally agile, you can feel emotions fully without being held captive by them. Bolstering your emotional agility will enable you to encounter stressful situations without falling back on unproductive emotional responses.

According to Dr. Susan David, a psychologist at Harvard Medical School and author of "Emotional Agility," recognizing and naming your emotions without judgment is crucial.

Emotions are perfectly okay; they are what make us human. Not allowing ourselves to be controlled by those emotions is a practice that we must master, and the first step is being able to name our feelings accurately.

Practical Steps to Enhance Emotional Agility:

> **1. Practice Mindfulness**
>
> Mindfulness involves paying attention to your thoughts and feelings without judgment. This can be achieved through meditation, deep-breathing exercises, or simply taking a moment to pause and reflect during your day. By cultivating mindfulness, you become more aware of your emotional state, making it easier to manage your reactions.
>
> **Actionable Step:** Spend 10 minutes each day practicing mindfulness. Sit quietly, focus on your breath, and gently bring your mind back when it starts to wander.
>
> **2. Label Your Emotions**

When you experience a strong emotion, take a moment to identify and name it. Are you feeling angry, frustrated, anxious, or sad? Labeling your emotions helps to create a mental distance between you and the feeling, making it easier to address and manage.

Actionable Step: Keep a journal where you regularly write down your emotions. Describe the situation that triggered the feeling and the name of the emotion you experienced.

3. Accept Your Emotions

Acceptance does not mean resignation. Instead, it means acknowledging your emotions without trying to suppress or deny them. This acceptance is a crucial step toward understanding and managing your emotions effectively.

Actionable Step: When you notice a difficult emotion, silently tell yourself, "It's okay to feel this way." Allow yourself a few moments to sit with the emotion without trying to change it.

4. Challenge Your Thoughts

Our emotions are often driven by the stories we tell ourselves. By challenging these stories, you can alter your emotional responses. Ask yourself if your thoughts are based on facts or assumptions and consider alternative perspectives.

Actionable Step: Next time you feel a negative emotion, write down the thoughts running through your mind. Then, challenge each thought by asking, "Is this true? Can I think of another explanation?"

5. Develop Emotional Flexibility

Emotional agility involves being able to shift your perspective and approach different situations with flexibility. This means being open to new experiences and willing to adapt your mindset as needed.

Actionable Step: Try something new that challenges your usual way of thinking. This could be reading a book on a topic you're unfamiliar with, trying a new hobby, or engaging in a conversation with someone who has a different viewpoint.

6. Cultivate Compassion

Compassion for yourself and others can greatly enhance emotional agility. When you approach your emotions and those of others with kindness and understanding, it becomes easier to navigate emotional challenges.

Actionable Step: Practice self-compassion by speaking to yourself as you would to a friend in need. When others express their emotions, listen without judgment and offer your support.

By incorporating these practices into your daily life, you can develop greater emotional agility, enabling you to handle life's challenges with resilience and grace. Remember, enhancing emotional agility is a continuous process that requires patience and commitment, but the rewards are well worth the effort.

The Practice of Letting Go

Letting go is perhaps the most challenging aspect of caring not to care. You must consciously release the desire to control outcomes, the need for approval, and the fear of uncertainty.

Take, for example, Mahatma Gandhi, who maintained his focus on long-term goals despite the many trials he faced. Gandhi's commitment to nonviolence and his unwavering belief in the power of peaceful resistance exemplify the essence of letting go. He had to release his desire to control every immediate outcome, trusting instead in the larger vision of freedom and justice for his people.

This ability to let go of the need to manage every detail and to find acceptance in the journey itself enabled him to inspire a movement that transcended immediate obstacles.

Gandhi's approach teaches us that letting go is not about giving up; it is about understanding and accepting that not all variables can be controlled. It is about finding strength in patience and perseverance, knowing that the path to achieving significant change is often unpredictable and fraught with setbacks. By letting go of the need for immediate validation and the fear of uncertain outcomes, we open ourselves to a deeper level of resilience and creativity, allowing our true purpose to guide us through challenges.

Creating a Followership of Trust

Cultivating a network of trusted followers is essential for effective leadership and personal growth, especially when it comes to the ability to let go. Trust forms the foundation upon which strong relationships are built, enabling leaders to delegate responsibilities and release control without fear. By surrounding yourself with individuals who believe in your vision and are committed to your success, you create a supportive environment that furthers mutual respect and collaboration.

Trusted followers are not just passive supporters; they actively engage, provide valuable insights, and ensure that tasks are handled competently. Establishing this trust requires consistent effort, transparent communication, and a genuine commitment to the well-being and development of each team member. With a strong network of trusted followers, leaders can confidently let go, knowing that their vision and goals are in capable hands.

The following key elements highlight the importance of trust in enabling leaders to effectively delegate and release control.

>**Support and Encouragement:** Surround yourself with individuals who genuinely care about your well-being and

success. Trusted followers can offer advice, motivation, and reassurance, helping you to persevere and stay focused on your goals.

Effective Communication: Trust fosters open and honest conversations, leading to better collaboration and idea-sharing. Trusted followers are more inclined to give you constructive feedback, essential for personal and professional growth.

Enhanced Accountability: When there is mutual trust, there is a shared understanding of expectations and responsibilities. This minimizes conflicts and misunderstandings, ensuring efficient and effective teamwork.

Increased Influence and Leadership Effectiveness: Trust builds credibility and respect, crucial for effective leadership. Trusted followers are more willing to support your vision and efforts, contributing to overall success.

Positive Organizational Culture: Trust creates a sense of belonging and loyalty among followers, enhancing morale and job satisfaction. A positive culture retains talent and attracts new individuals aligned with your values and goals.

Focus on effort, not outcome. Trust not only strengthens relationships but also empowers leaders to delegate with confidence, knowing their vision is supported by capable and committed individuals. By adopting support and encouragement, maintaining open communication, enhancing accountability, and building a positive organizational culture, leaders can create an environment where mutual respect and collaboration thrive. This foundation of trust is key to achieving greater influence, leadership effectiveness, and overall success.

Building Resilience Through Non-Attachment

Non-attachment is a state of grace that enables you to fully engage with life without being attached to specific outcomes. Non-attachment means doing your best while understanding that many factors influencing the final result are beyond your control.

Research from mindfulness practices shows that non-attachment can significantly reduce stress and increase resilience. A study published in the journal "*Mindfulness*" found that individuals who practiced non-attachment experienced lower levels of stress and higher levels of well-being.

- **Celebrate Effort Over Achievement:** Recognize and reward the effort, both in yourself and others, as much as the achievements.
- **Learn from Every Outcome:** You can find a lesson in every outcome, regardless of whether you succeeded or failed. Focus on learning as the objective measure of value.

The Concept of "Caring Not to Care"

Now, let's explore the idea of "caring not to care." This might sound counterintuitive, but in a leadership context, it can be profoundly impactful. It means focusing on what truly matters and letting go of unnecessary worries and micromanagement. By caring about the big picture and trusting your team to handle the details, you adopt an environment of trust and autonomy.

Outcomes:

- **Increased Innovation:** When leaders step back and give employees the freedom to explore new ideas, innovation flourishes.
- **Enhanced Trust:** Trusting your team members to manage their tasks builds mutual respect and a stronger team dynamic.

- **Better Focus:** By not sweating the small stuff, leaders and team members can focus on strategic goals and personal growth.

Bringing It All Together - The Liberating Power of Care

Incorporating these practices not only enhances your workplace but also empowers you and your colleagues to grow both professionally and personally. Whether you're leading or following, by prioritizing growth, inclusivity, and development, and by understanding when to "care not to care," you can create a thriving, dynamic work environment.

In my career trajectory, nurturing the strength and vitality of the organization I am privileged to co-lead with my counter parts and direct upline leaders is always the focal point. This imperative arises from a multifaceted responsibility that encompasses the well-being and livelihoods of our dedicated workforce and extends to ensuring unparalleled satisfaction and fulfillment for our esteemed customers.

As a custodian of employee welfare, I am charged with fostering an environment that encourages growth, fosters inclusivity, and prioritizes professional development and personal fulfillment. Nourishing such an environment involves implementing policies that promote work-life balance, facilitate skill enhancement, and cultivate a culture of collaboration. Whether you're in a leadership position or part of a team, these principles are universally applicable.

Caring not to care is a liberating philosophy. Adopting this approach frees you from unnecessary burdens, allowing you to invest your energy where it counts. By practicing discernment, embracing emotional agility, learning to let go, and adopting resilience through non-attachment, you can navigate the complexities of leadership and life gracefully and effectively. This chapter is not a call to disengage but an invitation to engage more deeply and meaningfully with what truly matters.

Chapter 8: The Harmony of Spheres - Mastering Work-Life Balance

One early morning during our much-anticipated family vacation to Disney World, I found a quiet moment for reflection. This trip was special—it was our first family vacation since my son William was born and since the COVID-19 pandemic reshaped our lives. William, a sweet yet tenacious 4-year-old, came into the world just six months before the United States began wearing masks and sheltering in place.

My heart goes out to all those impacted by the pandemic. In some way, shape, or form, it touched every one of us. It also altered our perceptions of work-life balance and the value of personal time away from the office. I've come to realize that personal time doesn't look the same for everyone, and thus, neither does work-life balance.

As we began settling into our vacation bubble, I pondered the idea of slowing down—a stark contrast to what my son calls our typical "hurry, hurry" pace. Despite the challenges of keeping up with my determined toddler and often failing to match his energy level, I relished the opportunity to step back and enjoy the peace. There were no constant phone calls, no barrage of urgent emails, no crises demanding immediate attention, and no meetings to prepare for. Yet, even in this calm, I couldn't help but glance at my emails.

In a world where professionals, career seekers, and full-time family managers juggle work, life, family, and self-care, striving for balance can become overwhelming. Despite our quest for equilibrium, we often tilt toward imbalance. Feeling off-balance can create guilt, preventing us from fully enjoying our personal time, family moments, or self-care.

"Why am I stressing about balancing work and life to fit a model prescribed by others?" I wondered as I sat sipping my coffee from my Micky Mouse cup.

As I reflected, I realized that working brings me joy—and I don't feel bad about that. My family and my free time are also sources of pleasure, but why should I construct a work-life balance that doesn't feel true to me? After all, a musician composes a tune primarily for their own enjoyment; others eventually appreciate its elegance.

The Intricacies of Balance

In our pursuit of professional success and personal satisfaction, maintaining a work-life balance often presents itself as one of our most formidable challenges. This chapter delves into the intricate art of balancing the scales between our professional ambitions and the richness of our personal lives.

Work-life balance is a concept that is frequently discussed but often misunderstood. Many envision it as a perfect split between work and personal life, yet in reality, it is a fluid and dynamic state of equilibrium. This equilibrium does not demand a rigid partition of time and energy; instead, it seeks harmony where both facets of life coexist, each complementing and enhancing the other.

Achieving this balance involves recognizing that the demands of our professional and personal worlds are constantly shifting. There will be times when work demands more of our attention and periods when personal life takes precedence. The key lies in being adaptable and responsive to these shifts, ensuring that neither aspect consistently overshadows the other.

True work-life balance is about integration rather than separation. It's about finding ways to blend our professional duties with our personal passions and responsibilities seamlessly. This might mean setting clear boundaries to prevent work from encroaching on personal time, or it could involve finding joy and fulfillment in our work that transcends the traditional work-life divide.

Moreover, this balance contributes significantly to our overall sense of completeness and contentment. When we achieve a harmonious blend of work and life, we are more likely to experience a deeper satisfaction that stems from feeling whole and integrated. It allows us to bring our best selves to both our professional endeavors and our personal relationships, enriching each area with the strengths and insights gained from the other.

This chapter will explore strategies and practices to help you cultivate this dynamic equilibrium. From time management techniques to setting boundaries and finding joy in everyday activities, you will discover tools to navigate the complexities of balancing work and life. Through this journey, you will learn that balance is not a static goal but a continuous process of adjustment and realignment, ultimately leading to a more fulfilling and harmonious existence.

Redefining Work-Life Balance: A Personal Journey

Before we dive into my journey with work-life balance, I want to emphasize that what works for me may not work for everyone. My choices are tailored to how my brain functions and what I need to relax. This is not a cookie-cutter approach. My goal in this section is to share how I reached my point of acceptance and to encourage you to find what works best for you. If my way resonates with you, I hope my experiences help guide you. If not, I hope my story prompts you to consider what does work for you and set the necessary boundaries to create a harmonious work-life balance that makes sense for you.

Remember, what worked for you a year ago, five years ago, or ten years ago might not be the same for today. As our lives change, so must our work-life balance model.

In my quest for the "perfect" work-life balance, I've learned that balance is less about rigid structure and more about molding it to fit the ever-changing contours of life. I love my organization and often find myself working during vacations. This isn't due to corporate imposition or expectations from my leadership team but a personal choice. My leadership team, as well as my followership team, often stresses the importance of taking paid time off and enjoying it. They push back when I am online during paid time off (PTO), for which I am constantly grateful.

However, reviewing a few emails on vacation is not a sacrifice for me. It reflects my commitment to our 250 employees and ensures the well-being of our members, all while supporting my peace of mind. Reading and replying to a few emails while the rest of the household is still asleep means I don't worry about returning to a mountain of messages.

And as a leader, it's important to set expectations for your followers. For example, while I might answer emails during PTO, I do not expect my team to do the same. When on PTO, it is critical to ensure your team takes the time they are owed, unplug, and be free from the stressors of office life. Make sure you discuss this with your teams frequently, be open-minded to their work-life balance ideas, and above all, ensure they understand that while you, as the leader, may take actions during PTO or after normal business hours, this is not the standard or expectation. If you choose to work outside of normal business hours, you must consistently stress that it is your personal choice and not a requirement for your teams.

While my approach works for me, I must highlight that reviewing emails during PTO doesn't necessarily mean answering them. I might move junk emails, flag follow-ups, or categorize informational messages. The risk of answering emails during PTO is that you might set directions, ask questions, or create uncertainty that requires clarification. If your team or organization responds and you have closed your computer for the day, you may create more harm than good. If there is an emergency, I urge you to pick up the phone to ensure the right expectations are set and to clarify your availability.

I choose to review and organize my emails in the early morning of my PTO days as it relieves the stress of returning to a chaotic inbox and the added stress of feeling behind for a week or two post-vacation. I feel accomplished and relaxed knowing that when I return to the office, my emails will be in a manageable state.

That said, as my life changes and continues to change, I must pause and reflect on this approach. I have never completely disconnected while on PTO. Perhaps I should try it, to see if it creates a better experience. It's all about finding the right balance.

Trials and Tribulations: Mastering Work-Life Balance in a Modern Workforce

Our professional landscape features a unique blend of work-life balances and hybrid models. The art of managing PTO is essential, combining responsibility and self-care. We must orchestrate our absences with finesse, ensuring our teams manage our responsibilities without micromanaging them. Consistency is key; sporadic involvement can disrupt the rhythm, creating confusion and unrealistic expectations within our teams.

Although I check email while on vacation, I've learned the importance of setting clear boundaries. The siren song of morning emails can be enticing. However, clear communication with your leader and team is pivotal for ensuring you make the most of your PTO. Whether you fully unplug or occasionally peek at your inbox for peace of mind, coordinating with an acting leader ensures seamless communication and maintains productivity across the team.

However, there is much more to work-life balance than PTO. In fact, some might say that work-life balance doesn't really exist while on PTO. Paid Time Off should be much more about life than work. The balance while on PTO should be 99% about life. The one hour in the morning I spend reviewing emails might exceed that 99% a bit, but it's critical that the balance while on PTO is personal.

Beyond grand vacations, work-life balance extends significantly into daily life. In fact, work-life balance is more about finding harmony in your day-to-day activities than during one or two long PTO stretches.

As leaders and followers, it is crucial to be open to the changes in our world regarding work-life balance. While not all industries can implement all these suggestions, the goal is not to mirror exactly what I am writing but to advance openness, understanding, and support for our followers in achieving their own work-life balance. Involving your Human Resources team is vital if you are going well outside your organization's business hours or making extreme accommodations. They can support whether the organization can handle this as a whole and, if not, help find the right option to support the employee, or yourself.

That said, organizations must be open to the ever-changing ideas of work-life balance. For example, with the increasing costs of childcare, elder care, travel expenses, and more, many may be constantly worried about picking up the kids or making it to a doctor's appointment in the middle of the day.

Here are some work-life balance items to consider as you lead your organization forward:

- **Flexibility in Work Hours to Accommodate Personal Commitments:** Offering flexible work hours can significantly enhance work-life balance. This flexibility might include staggered start and end times, compressed work weeks, or the ability to shift hours to accommodate personal appointments and family responsibilities, without the need to burn through PTO. By allowing employees to tailor their work schedules, you acknowledge their diverse needs and help reduce stress related to rigid work hours. For instance, a parent may need to start work later to drop off their children at school or finish early to attend a child's soccer game. Flexibility shows trust in your employees' ability to manage their time effectively while meeting their work commitments.

- **Opportunities for Remote Work to Reduce Commuting Stress:** Remote work can be a game-changer for work-life balance, particularly in reducing the time and stress associated with commuting. Offering remote work options, whether full-time, part-time, or on specific days, can greatly enhance an employee's quality of life. It allows for more time with family, increased productivity due to a quieter environment, and the ability to work from any location. This flexibility can lead to higher job satisfaction and retention. For example, an employee who lives far from the office might save hours each week by working from home, allowing them to invest that time in personal activities or family. As well as be more acceptable to working past normal business hours on occasion to support projects, staffing limitations or emergencies.

- **Support for Continuing Education and Professional Development:** Encouraging and supporting continuing education and professional development helps employees grow their skills and advance their careers while encouraging a culture of lifelong learning. This support might include providing access to online courses, workshops, and seminars, or offering tuition reimbursement programs. By investing in their development, you empower employees to achieve their career goals and stay motivated. Additionally, allowing time within the work schedule for these activities shows that you value their growth and are willing to support their aspirations. For instance, an employee may wish to pursue a certification relevant to their field, and having the organization's backing can make this endeavor less burdensome and more rewarding. Consider providing said employee an hour or 2 a week for this study on "business hours."

Personal Anecdote Time: I remember my first corporate office position working for a medium-sized bank. I had an associate degree and was pursuing my bachelor's. My financial situation required a full-time position (or more) to ensure I could contribute to my spouse's and my living expenses. While the bank I worked for did provide some tuition assistance, I'll be honest: the few thousand dollars a year would have been more beneficial if my organization had said, "You know, three days a week between 11-12 will be your study time. Use this on-the-clock time to help complete your studies toward your degree."

This would have provided me with a dedicated time slot during business hours to focus on my courses and materials, reducing the after-work and weekend time needed for schoolwork. This approach would have demonstrated that my organization cared not only about my pursuit of continuing education but also about my work-life balance. It would have given me valuable personal time back during non-business hours that would otherwise have been required for my studies. Providing more rest and recovery time, to come back to work the next business day in a better frame of mind, therefore providing better results.

I'll be honest, I never asked my organization at the time if I could do this. I was young, didn't want to seem ungrateful for having a job, and didn't fully understand the concept of work-life balance. The point here is that as leaders, we must recognize that our employees may not ask for what is not considered societally acceptable. Especially with young employees who may be more timid in asking for a little extra in the form of work-life balance or time.

As we, who held full-time positions and pursued full-time educational advancement, climb the leadership ranks, remember the challenges you faced. Use your success to determine if your organization can offer work-life balance in the form of time to support your employees in furthering their education. There are about 2,000 hours in a working year. College time frames are about 7 months of said year. College semesters typically span about seven months of that year. If you allow your employees three hours a week for college study during those seven months, that will total 84 hours, or roughly 4% of the working year. That's a tuition reimbursement if I've ever heard of one.

While leaders play a crucial role in setting the stage for a healthy work-life balance, followers also have responsibilities and opportunities to create their own balance. Here are some actions followers can take:

- **Communicate Needs Clearly:** Share your personal commitments and work-life balance needs with your leader. Open and honest communication ensures mutual understanding and support.

- **Utilize Available Resources:** Take advantage of any flexible work options, remote work opportunities, and professional development programs offered by your organization.

- **Set Personal Boundaries:** Establish clear boundaries between work and personal life. For example, decide not to check work emails after a certain hour or during family time.

- **Plan and Prioritize:** Organize your tasks and responsibilities to ensure that you are meeting both work and personal commitments. Prioritize your workload to avoid last-minute stress and overtime.

- **Seek Support:** Don't hesitate to ask for help when needed, whether from colleagues, supervisors, or the HR department. Utilizing available support can help manage workload and reduce stress.

- **Take Regular Breaks:** Ensure you take short breaks throughout the workday to recharge. This can help maintain productivity and mental well-being.

- **Engage in Self-Care:** Make time for activities that promote relaxation and well-being, such as exercise, hobbies, and spending time with loved ones.

Followers should embrace their role in shaping their work-life balance, approaching it with the same adaptability and openness as leaders. By actively participating in this journey, they can create a sustainable and fulfilling work-life harmony.

Embracing Our Unique Work-Life Symphony

As the sun rose on another day of my vacation, casting a golden hue over the Magic Kingdom, I realized that our quest for work-life balance is like an artist's journey—unique, always evolving, and deeply personal.

The epiphany I experienced amidst the tranquility of this family retreat is that balance is not a rigid template to be universally applied but a fluid melody that each of us composes based on the rhythm of our lives.

For Leaders: Leaders often face the challenge of setting an example while managing their own work-life balance. They must navigate the fine line between being available for their team and taking time for themselves. Leaders should prioritize clear communication, delegate effectively, and trust their teams to manage responsibilities. This involves setting boundaries and being transparent about their own practices, such as checking emails during PTO but not expecting the same from their team. By modeling healthy work-life balance habits, leaders can create a culture that values and supports this balance.

As a leader, what strategies are you implementing or considering promoting work-life balance? Are you effectively communicating these initiatives to your teams and followers?

For Followers: Followers, or team members, should feel empowered to advocate for their work-life balance needs. This includes communicating openly with their leaders about personal commitments and utilizing the resources and flexibility offered by the organization. Followers should also set their own boundaries, such as not checking work emails after hours, to ensure they have time to recharge. Actively participating in discussions about work-life balance can help followers contribute to a supportive work environment.

As a team member, are there work-life balance challenges you are striving to overcome? Have you communicated these concerns to your leaders?

Full-Time Employees: Full-time employees often have more structured schedules but may also have access to more comprehensive benefits and resources for work-life balance. They should take advantage of flexible work hours, remote work opportunities, and professional development programs to create a balance that works for them. Full-time employees can also benefit from regular check-ins with their managers to discuss workload and balance, ensuring they are not overburdened.

Part-Time Employees: Part-time employees might have more flexibility in their schedules but may face challenges such as less access to benefits or feeling disconnected from full-time colleagues. It's important for part-time employees to communicate their availability clearly and make the most of their work hours to maintain productivity. They should also seek to engage with their teams and participate in professional development opportunities when possible, to feel more integrated and supported.

Contractors: Contractors often have the most flexibility but also the least job security and benefits. They must be proactive in managing their work-life balance, setting clear boundaries with clients about availability and work hours. Contractors should also prioritize self-care and continuous learning to stay competitive in their field. Networking with other professionals and seeking out supportive communities can provide additional resources and support for maintaining a healthy balance.

Ultimately, the key to achieving work-life balance is recognizing that it is a personal and dynamic process. Each individual's balance will look different based on their role, employment type, and personal circumstances. By approaching work-life balance as a fluid melody rather than a rigid template, we can all create a harmonious rhythm that suits our unique lives.

In the current professional landscape, where the lines between work and personal life blur, we must recognize that the traditional notion of balance might not suit everyone. Just as a musician harmonizes various notes to create a symphony, we, too, must find harmony in the diverse aspects of our lives. The key is not in segregating but in integrating work, family, and self-care in a way that resonates with our individual needs and values.

Checking a few emails during my vacation morning routine isn't a breach of work-life balance: it's an integral part of my harmony. Doing so ensures peace of mind, allowing me to be fully present with my family for the rest of the day. This approach may not align with everyone, and that's okay. The beauty lies in the diversity of our melodies.

I urge leaders and organizations to create a culture of flexibility and understanding. Recognize that each member of your team has a unique symphony to compose. Support them in finding their rhythm, and in turn, they will perform with greater harmony and dedication.

Intermission Break – We've covered a substantial amount in this chapter. Now might be an ideal moment to take a break, reflect, and assimilate what we've discussed so far.

If you chose to take a break. Wonderful! Here is a quick recap:

For Leaders and Organizations:

- **Foster Open Communication:** Encourage open dialogue about work-life balance. Create a safe space where team members feel comfortable discussing their needs and challenges without fear of judgment or repercussion. Regular check-ins and feedback sessions can help leaders understand individual preferences and adjust support accordingly.

- **Offer Flexibility:** Implement flexible work policies that cater to diverse needs. This can include options for remote work, flexible working hours, compressed workweeks, and part-time arrangements. Flexibility demonstrates trust in your employees and acknowledges their need to balance professional and personal responsibilities.

- **Lead by Example:** Model healthy work-life balance behaviors. When leaders take time off and respect their own boundaries, it sets a powerful example for the team. Show that it's acceptable—and encouraged—to disconnect and recharge.

- **Provide Resources and Support:** Offer resources that support work-life balance, such as wellness programs, mental health services, and professional development opportunities. Providing access to tools and programs that promote well-being can significantly enhance your team's ability to manage stress and maintain balance.

- **Celebrate Diversity in Work Styles:** Understand that work-life balance looks different for everyone. Some may prefer a clear separation between work and home life, while others might find peace in blending the two. Respect and accommodate these differences, promoting an environment where everyone can thrive.

- **Encourage Time Off:** Promote the importance of taking PTO and ensuring it is truly time away from work. Discourage the culture of always being "on" and celebrate the rejuvenation that comes from a proper break.

For Fellow Professionals:

- **Embrace Fluidity:** Understand that work-life balance is not a one-size-fits-all solution. It is a dynamic process that evolves with your personal and professional growth. Be open to adjusting your approach as your circumstances change.

- **Set Personal Boundaries:** Clearly define when and how you will engage with work, especially during personal time. Whether it's not checking emails after a certain hour or fully unplugging during vacations, set boundaries that help you recharge.

- **Communicate Needs:** Don't hesitate to express your work-life balance needs to your leaders and colleagues. Clear communication helps build a supportive environment where everyone's needs are respected.

- **Find Your Rhythm:** Identify what work-life balance looks like for you. Whether it's starting your day with a quick email check or completely disconnecting during weekends, find what brings you peace and stick to it.

- **Engage in Self-Care:** Prioritize activities that promote your physical, mental, and emotional well-being. Regular exercise, hobbies, time with loved ones, and relaxation are crucial components of a balanced life.

- **Stay Adaptable:** As your life changes, so too should your approach to work-life balance. Regularly reassess your needs and be willing to make adjustments to maintain harmony in your life.

The Symphony of Life

Remember, a well-composed life, like a beautiful symphony, resonates within ourselves and inspires those around us. When we find our own rhythm and respect the rhythms of others, we create a harmonious environment where everyone can perform at their best. Embrace the fluidity of your work-life composition, and together, let's create a culture where balance is not just a goal but a shared reality.

As I returned to the joy of my vacation, my son's laughter echoing against the backdrop of Cinderella's Castle, I was reminded that life, in all its complexity, is a beautiful composition. Let us each find our rhythm, compose our symphonies, and play them passionately. Ultimately, it is not the balance we strike but the harmony we create that defines the richness of our lives.

Strategies for Harmonizing Work and Life

Achieving work-life balance is a continuous journey that requires thoughtful consideration and deliberate actions. In our fast-paced, digitally connected world, it's easy to feel overwhelmed by the demands of both professional and personal life. However, by adopting specific strategies and making conscious choices, we can create a harmonious blend that enhances our well-being and productivity. Here are some practical strategies to help you harmonize work and life effectively:

- **Practice the Art of Prioritization:** Understanding what we value in both personal and professional realms is a cornerstone of work-life balance. Prioritizing tasks and commitments based on their impact ensures optimal use of time and energy. Begin by identifying your most critical tasks and allocate time for them first. Use tools like to-do lists, calendars, and priority matrices to keep track of what needs immediate attention and what can wait. Learning to say no to non-essential tasks can also help maintain focus on what truly matters.

- **Redraw the Boundaries:** Setting clear boundaries is essential in an age where constant connectivity is the norm. Practical ways to delineate work and personal time include setting specific work hours and sticking to them, creating a dedicated workspace at home, and turning off work notifications during personal time. Communicate these boundaries to colleagues and family members to ensure everyone understands and respects them. Taking regular breaks throughout the day and having a clear end-of-day routine can also help signal the transition from work to personal time.

- **Embrace Self-Care:** The significance of self-care in maintaining balance cannot be overstated. Engaging in activities that rejuvenate the mind and body is vital. Hobbies, exercise, and mindfulness practices can counterbalance work-related stress. Schedule regular time for activities you enjoy, whether it's reading, gardening, playing a sport, or meditating. Physical activities like yoga, jogging, or even a short walk can significantly reduce stress levels. Mindfulness practices such as "My Meditation" or even quick deep-breathing exercises can help clear your mind and improve focus.

- **Add in the Flexibility Factor:** The modern workplace often offers flexibility in terms of hours and location. Leveraging this flexibility can be a powerful tool in achieving a better balance, making it possible to accommodate personal and professional responsibilities more effectively. If your job allows, consider flexible working hours that align better with your personal life. Remote work can reduce commuting time and provide a more comfortable work environment. Discuss with your employer the possibility of a hybrid model if it suits your role and responsibilities.

- **Reflect and Adapt:** Work-life balance is not a one-time achievement but an ongoing process. Striking the right balance requires regular adjustment to align with changing life circumstances and career phases. Periodically reflect on your current balance and assess whether it meets your needs. Life changes, such as a new job, the birth of a child, or a change in health, may necessitate a reevaluation of your priorities and boundaries. Be flexible and willing to adapt your strategies to find a balance that works for you at different stages of your life.

By implementing these strategies, you can create a harmonious blend of work and personal life that enhances overall well-being and productivity. Remember, achieving work-life balance is a dynamic process that requires continuous effort and adjustment.

Individual Variability in Work-Life Balance

Achieving work-life balance is a highly individualized process. What constitutes balance for one person may not hold for another. This variability stems from numerous factors, including career goals, family responsibilities, personal health, and social commitments. Self-reflection will help you understand your unique priorities and constraints. Regularly assessing your values and goals can guide you in making decisions that align with your definition of balance.

Strategies for Self-Reflection:

- **Daily Journaling:** Spend a few minutes each day writing about your experiences, feelings, and thoughts. This practice can help you identify patterns in your work-life balance and recognize areas that need adjustment.

- **Set Aside Quiet Time:** Dedicate a specific time each week to sit quietly and reflect on your life. Consider what is working well and what isn't. Ask yourself questions like, "Am I spending enough time on what truly matters to me?" and "What changes can I make to improve my balance?"

- **Periodic Goal Review:** Regularly review your personal and professional goals. Ensure they align with your current values and circumstances. Adjust your goals as needed to reflect any changes in your priorities or life situation.

- **Seek Feedback:** Talk to trusted friends, family members, or colleagues about your work-life balance. Their insights can provide a different perspective and help you identify blind spots.

- **Mindfulness Practices:** Engage in mindfulness activities such as "My Meditation". These practices can help you become more aware of your thoughts and feelings, allowing for deeper self-reflection and understanding.

When faced with overwhelming demands from work and personal life, employ strategies to help mitigate stress. Techniques such as prioritizing tasks based on urgency and importance, practicing time-blocking to focus on specific activities, and embracing the power of delegation can all contribute to a more manageable daily routine. Incorporating relaxation practices like deep breathing exercises or short meditative breaks can help reset your focus and reduce anxiety.

Leveraging Technology for Balance

When used mindfully, technology can be an ally in achieving work-life balance. Tools like time management apps (e.g., Toggl, RescueTime) can help you see how you spend your time and identify areas for improvement. Meanwhile, apps designed to limit screen time (e.g., Freedom, Forest) can encourage more meaningful engagement with the world around you. Customizing notification settings to minimize distractions during family time or personal activities can also help maintain boundaries between work and personal life.

Cultural Considerations in Work-Life Balance

Cultural influences also shape our approach to work-life balance. For instance, in cultures with a strong emphasis on communal values and family time, balance might include more family-oriented activities and community engagement. Conversely, in cultures where professional achievement is highly valued, finding a balance may involve setting more explicit boundaries around work to protect personal time. Understanding and respecting these cultural dimensions can enhance the effectiveness of work-life balance strategies.

Concluding Thoughts: Cultivating Harmony

Work-life balance is a personal and professional imperative. It is a dynamic, ever-evolving journey unique to each individual. We all have a responsibility to identify our needs and limitations and take proactive steps toward achieving a fulfilling and balanced life.

Ultimately, work-life balance is about creating a life where work and personal life coexist harmoniously, enriching each other. Work-life balance is not a static equilibrium but rather a dynamic interplay between competing demands. Prioritization and boundary setting are essential, and we can access the rejuvenating power of self-care and the flexibility of modern work arrangements to aid our journey toward balance.

Balance is not a one-size-fits-all concept. We each embark on a unique journey shaped by our aspirations, cultural norms, and life circumstances. The journey offers immense rewards for personal fulfillment and professional effectiveness. Let us embrace the fluidity of balance and celebrate the resilience of the human spirit. Let us strive not for perfection but for harmony—a life where work and personal pursuits coexist.

We can continue cultivating harmony in our lives, one step at a time, knowing that the pursuit of balance is not just a destination but a lifelong journey toward a more enriching existence.

Chapter 9: Changing Hands

In the constantly evolving landscape of the modern workplace, leaders must effectively manage a workforce composed of various generations, from the experienced Baby Boomers to the digitally native Generation Z. As technology continues to shape our work environment, leaders face the dual challenges of integrating these technological advances and blending the distinct traits of each generation into a unified, productive team. This chapter explores successful cross-generational leadership strategies, advancing an inclusive and dynamic work culture.

Some fundamental components essential for harmonizing a diverse, multi-generational workforce involve discovering common ground and thoughtfully investing time in understanding each generation's motivations. Bringing common denominators to light among our teams can help us illuminate a middle ground.

Understanding and adopting followership is critical in any professional setting. Whether you are a young professional just starting your career or a seasoned professional well-established in your field, learning to follow one another and creating a give-and-take relationship is essential. This mutual respect and cooperation will be the driving force behind the success of cross-generational teams, which are now present at almost every level of any organization.

As leaders, we must emphasize to all who report to us, regardless of their age or experience level, the importance of followership. Both the youth and mature professionals need to understand the value of following one another.

For mature professionals, this means being open to new ideas, accepting questions from the youth, and adopting emerging technologies. It requires a willingness to adapt and learn from the fresh perspectives that younger colleagues bring. On the other hand, young professionals need to follow the wisdom that comes from years of experience. They should appreciate the art of mastering a craft, the importance of stability, and the nuanced charm that often comes with experience.

By embracing followership, young professionals can make smoother transitions and learn to balance innovation with time-tested practices. Meanwhile, mature professionals can stay relevant and invigorated by integrating new methodologies and insights. Ultimately, this reciprocal relationship creates a dynamic and cohesive team, capable of navigating the complexities of the modern workplace with both grace and efficiency.

Understanding Generational Differences

Generational cohorts are a fascinating way to understand the evolution of society, each with its unique tapestry woven by the threads of shared experiences and defining moments. Let's explore these generational groups, as often defined by sociologists, historians, and demographers, to identify the remarkable people born during distinct periods and their distinctive characteristics:

The Greatest Generation (GI Generation):

- Born: 1901-1927
- Characteristics: This resilient group grew up during the Great Depression and fought valiantly in World War II. Known for their unwavering sense of duty, frugality, and perseverance, they laid the groundwork for the modern era with their sacrifices and steadfastness.

The Silent Generation:

- Born: 1928-1945
- Characteristics: Coming of age during World War II and the austere post-war period, this generation is often noted for their cautious nature, loyalty, and adherence to traditional values. Their quiet strength and commitment provided a stabilizing force during times of upheaval.

Baby Boomers:

- Born: 1946-1964
- Characteristics: Born amidst the post-World War II baby boom, this generation basked in an era of economic prosperity. Marked by their optimism and a relentless pursuit of personal success, Baby Boomers shaped the cultural landscape with their dynamic and ambitious spirit.

Generation X:

- Born: 1965-1980

- Characteristics: Navigating the shift from the industrial age to the digital era, Generation X is known for its independence, skepticism, and a profound emphasis on work-life balance. This pragmatic cohort values self-reliance and innovation, often acting as a bridge between traditional and modern sensibilities.

Millennials (Generation Y):

- Born: 1981-1996
- Characteristics: Coming of age during the internet explosion, Millennials are characterized by their technological savviness and social consciousness. They prioritize experiences over possessions and are known for their adaptability and commitment to making a positive impact on the world.

Generation Z:

- Born: 1997-2012
- Characteristics: As true digital natives, Generation Z grew up with smartphones and social media as integral parts of their lives. Valuing diversity and demonstrating a pragmatic approach to life, they are poised to lead with their innovative ideas and global perspective.

Generation Alpha:

- Born: 2013-Present
- Characteristics: The first generation entirely born in the 21st century, Generation Alpha is growing up in an unprecedentedly technological and interconnected world. They are anticipated to be the most educated and digitally proficient generation, ready to shape the future with their unique perspectives and advanced skills.

Each generation, with its distinctive traits and experiences, contributes to the rich and complex narrative of our collective history. Understanding these groups helps us appreciate the diverse tapestry of human progress and the enduring spirit that propels us forward.

Effective leadership hinges on a nuanced understanding of the distinctive characteristics each generation brings to the table. For instance, Baby Boomers are celebrated for their loyalty and strong work ethic, Generation X emphasizes work-life balance, while Millennials place a high value on flexibility and purpose, and Gen Z is known for its entrepreneurial spirit and tech-savviness.

However, it's essential to recognize that these values are not confined to a single generation. Instead, they represent a cumulative process where each generation integrates its unique expectations and values while also appreciating the contributions of the others. This blending of traits creates a dynamic and diverse workplace culture.

Acknowledging these generational traits is crucial for developing strategies that resonate with each group. By leveraging the extensive experience of Baby Boomers and the technological adeptness of Gen Z, and everything in between, leaders can create innovative solutions and enhance problem-solving. Embracing the strengths of each generation not only enriches the work environment but also drives collective success.

Adapting Communication Strategies

Tailoring communication styles to each generation is essential for effective cross-generational leadership. Traditional face-to-face meetings may resonate more with experienced generations, while younger professionals often prefer digital platforms. Leaders must employ versatile communication strategies to ensure inclusivity, adopting an environment where everyone feels valued and understood.

Educating each generation on the value of various communication methods encourages mutual understanding and adaptability. Just as we learn to respect and honor the customs and traditions of different ethnic and cultural backgrounds, we must also appreciate and convey our own beliefs and practices. This approach shows respect, safeguards beliefs, and facilitates meaningful interactions.

We need to respect and understand that everyone often has their own preferred way of communicating. This understanding is equally applicable in cross-generational interactions. For instance, while explaining the significance and added value of face-to-face meetings, it is equally important to encourage experienced generations to embrace technological advancements. Finding a balanced approach that integrates both traditional and modern communication methods is key.

The cornerstone of successful cross-generational leadership lies in building trust and nurturing open, honest communication about generational differences. By encouraging an environment of respect and adaptability, leaders can bridge the gap between generations, harnessing the strengths of each to drive collective success.

Steps to Accomplish Effective Cross-Generational Communication:

1. **Assess Preferences and Needs:**
    - Conduct surveys or informal discussions to understand the preferred communication styles of your team members.

2. **Leverage Multiple Channels:**
    - Use a mix of communication platforms, such as emails, instant messaging apps, video

conferences, and face-to-face meetings, to cater to diverse preferences.
- Implement flexible communication tools that allow for both synchronous and asynchronous interactions.

3. **Provide Training and Support:**
    - Offer training sessions to help all team members become proficient with new communication technologies and platforms.
    - Encourage experienced generations to mentor younger colleagues on traditional communication methods and vice versa.

4. **Adopt an Open Dialogue:**
    - Create forums or regular meetings where team members can discuss communication preferences and suggest improvements.
    - Promote a culture of feedback where everyone feels comfortable sharing their thoughts on communication effectiveness.

5. **Encourage Empathy and Understanding:**
    - Organize workshops or team-building activities focused on generational diversity and the importance of understanding each other's communication styles.
    - Highlight the benefits of different communication methods, emphasizing how each can contribute to team success.

6. **Demonstrate Flexibility:**

- Show willingness to adapt your own communication style to meet the needs of different generations.
- Encourage leaders and managers to model this behavior, demonstrating flexibility and openness.

7. **Balance Tradition and Innovation:**
   - Explain the significance and added value of face-to-face meetings, particularly for building relationships and trust.
   - Simultaneously, promote the use of digital tools for efficiency and convenience, helping experienced generations see their benefits.

8. **Measure and Adjust:**
   - Regularly evaluate the effectiveness of your communication strategies through feedback and performance metrics.
   - Be prepared to adjust your approach based on what works best for your team, remaining responsive to changing preferences.

A classic example is the preference for face-to-face communication versus virtual meetings. Younger generations might inquire why in-person meetings are valued so highly when virtual meetings seem more efficient. To this, senior generations could explain: "Indeed, virtual meetings are efficient, and we appreciate how younger generations have integrated this into our culture, transforming some meetings into swift virtual sessions. However, meetings are about more than just efficiency. They develop a sense of connection and a personal touch, allowing us to get to know each other, share laughter and jokes, and observe reactions we may not be able to see virtually. In-person meetings also minimize the distractions from various technological communication channels. By meeting face-to-face, we can focus more intently and dedicate ourselves to the conversation."

By taking these steps, leaders and followers can bridge the communication gap between generations, creating a more cohesive and productive work environment. This balanced approach not only respects the unique characteristics of each generation but also leverages their strengths, leading to innovative solutions and enhanced problem-solving.

As a leader, it is crucial to follow your teams' preferences in how they wish to be communicated with while also encouraging them to respect and occasionally adopt each other's communication styles. This mutual adaptation advances a collaborative and harmonious workplace where everyone's contributions are valued.

Reciprocal Mentoring

Mentorship is a vital tool for bridging generational divides, and leaders can consider employing both traditional and reverse mentoring strategies. Traditional mentoring enables younger employees to gain insights from the experiences of their seniors. In reverse mentoring, experienced staff members learn about new trends from more youthful colleagues. This bi-directional mentorship cultivates learning, respect, and understanding that can transcend generational barriers.

Many mentorship and leadership development programs are one-sided, primarily focusing on senior members instructing younger or newer leaders on the dos and don'ts. However, for these programs to be truly effective, they should be approached as a bi-directional exchange. Or Reciprocal Mentorship as I call it.

Traditional mentorship typically involves a mentor guiding a mentee. However, as we integrate multiple generations within the workplace, it's time to evolve from this conventional model to a more collaborative approach. This is where my philosophy of Reciprocal Mentoring comes into play.

In Reciprocal Mentoring, the traditional designations of mentor and mentee are dissolved, removing hierarchical power dynamics and placing everyone on equal footing. Each individual brings unique strengths and insights to the table, creating a balanced and mutually beneficial relationship. In this style of mentoring, both parties act as mentors and mentees simultaneously, creating a dynamic exchange of knowledge and experience.

Too often, traditional mentorship elevates the mentor while the mentee bears the brunt of the work. This approach can perpetuate a one-sided learning experience, which is not ideal for true growth and development. Reciprocal Mentoring, on the other hand, ensures that all generations see the benefits of both leading and following. By sharing responsibilities equally, participants learn the importance of adapting to both roles.

This method instills the value of flexibility and mutual respect, highlighting the significance of being both a follower and a leader. By embracing Reciprocal Mentoring, we cultivate a culture where every individual can contribute and learn, promoting a more inclusive and dynamic workplace.

The practice of reciprocal mentoring is especially vital for the younger generation, whose attitudes, expectations, and views on hierarchy often differ significantly from those of previous generations. The focus isn't on determining who is right or wrong, but on ensuring that both sides are heard. More importantly, it's about actively listening and integrating the diverse ideas from different generations into a cohesive dialogue.

The more experienced generations should guide and prepare the younger generation for the future. Eventually, the newest generations in the workforce will become the senior members and must adapt to the generations that follow them. If the more youthful generation now observes their seniors adapting, changing, and learning, this behavior will be ingrained in them, strengthening a culture of reciprocal learning and growth for all generations to come.

Beware of Generational Stereotypes

Understanding generational characteristics is crucial for effective leadership; however, it is equally important to avoid the trap of overgeneralization. Stereotypes can hinder our ability to see each team member's unique contributions and potential. For example, although it is common to label Baby Boomers as less tech-savvy or Gen Z as having shorter attention spans, these stereotypes do not reflect the capabilities of every person within these generational groups. Such broad generalizations can lead to misjudgments and missed opportunities for leveraging the strengths of individual team members.

To counteract generational stereotypes, leaders and followers should focus on individual interactions. This means taking the time to get to know each team member personally, understanding their strengths, weaknesses, and unique contributions. By doing so, leaders can recognize and nurture personal strengths and identify development opportunities tailored to each individual. This personalized approach not only helps in tapping into the full potential of the workforce but also develops a sense of value and respect among employees.

Furthermore, adopting a culture of open communication is essential. Leaders should encourage team members to share their experiences, skills, and perspectives. This can be achieved through regular team meetings, one-on-one check-ins, and informal gatherings that promote dialogue and understanding. When employees feel heard and understood, it breaks down the barriers of stereotypes and builds a more inclusive and cohesive team environment.

An inclusive work environment benefits greatly from the diverse talents and perspectives each generation brings to the table. For instance, Baby Boomers might offer extensive industry knowledge and a strong work ethic, while Millennials and Gen Z might bring fresh ideas and technological expertise. Recognizing and appreciating these diverse contributions can lead to more innovative problem-solving and a more dynamic workplace.

Training programs and workshops focused on generational diversity and inclusion can further educate team members about the pitfalls of stereotypes and the importance of embracing diversity. These initiatives can provide practical strategies for encouraging an inclusive culture and equip employees with the skills needed to collaborate effectively across generational lines.

Understanding generational characteristics is essential, but it must be balanced with an awareness of the dangers of stereotyping. By focusing on individual interactions, encouraging open communication, and promoting an inclusive culture, leaders can effectively leverage the diverse talents within their teams. This approach not only enhances team cohesion and morale but also drives innovation and productivity, ultimately leading to a more successful and harmonious workplace.

Flexible Policies and Inclusive Culture

A key factor in cross-generational workforce harmony is the implementation of flexible policies that cater to the diverse needs of each generation. These policies might include variable working hours, allowing employees to start and end their workday at times that best suit their personal and family obligations. Additionally, remote work options can accommodate those who prefer the flexibility of working from home, whether it's to reduce commuting time, better manage work-life balance, or simply to work in an environment where they feel most productive.

Furthermore, an inclusive culture that values and respects each generation's unique contributions is critical. For instance, while younger employees may bring fresh perspectives and digital fluency, older employees often offer invaluable experience and institutional knowledge. Recognizing and celebrating these strengths fosters an environment of mutual respect and learning.

To truly embrace diversity, organizations should promote open dialogue and actively encourage feedback from all age groups. This can be facilitated through regular team meetings, anonymous suggestion submissions, or even collaborative projects where diverse teams work together to solve problems and innovate. Such initiatives not only enhance team unity but also boost overall morale, as employees feel heard and valued regardless of their age.

For example, creating intergenerational task forces to tackle specific challenges can leverage the unique strengths of each age group, creating a spirit of collaboration and mutual respect. Additionally, organizing social events and team-building activities that appeal to a wide range of interests can help break down barriers and build stronger interpersonal relationships. Please do these during regular business hours as much as possible.

By integrating these flexible and inclusive approaches, organizations can create a balanced and productive work environment where all generations thrive and contribute their best.

Practicing What You Preach

While having appropriate policies and practices in place is necessary, it is not sufficient on its own. Leaders must fully embrace these policies and understand the nuances of effectively managing multi-generational teams. This involves setting clear expectations, accurately assessing performance, engaging in challenging conversations, and genuinely understanding how to empower and sustain motivation among team members. This is a cornerstone in being The Leader & The Follower. As a leader, you must adhere to the principles and guidelines your organization has established. Demonstrating that you can follow the lead is one of the easiest ways to gain buy-in and prove your effectiveness as a leader. By embodying the policies and procedures you expect others to follow, you illustrate your commitment and ability to lead by example. If a practice needs to be changed, showing that you are currently following the existing procedure is the best way to advocate for improvement.

Too often, we encounter practices that need updating or overhauling. Unfortunately, when these practices as they are at the moment are not adhered to by leadership, it undermines the credibility of calls for change. Leaders might acknowledge the existence of a process but fail to follow it themselves, which weakens their position when advocating for improvements.

This issue is particularly relevant in the context of cross-generational leadership. Leaders often speak about the importance of open dialogue and equality yet fail to demonstrate these principles in practice. For example, they may emphasize the need for transparent communication and mutual respect among team members of different ages, but if they do not personally engage in these behaviors, their words ring hollow.

To truly create an environment of open dialogue and equality, leaders must lead by example. This means actively participating in the processes they promote, whether it's maintaining open lines of communication, respecting diverse perspectives, or fairly assessing performance across all age groups. By embodying the values they espouse, leaders not only build trust and credibility but also create a culture where all employees feel valued and heard.

Moreover, when leaders consistently follow established practices, it provides a solid foundation for advocating changes when necessary. If a particular practice proves to be ineffective or outdated, leaders who have adhered to it can more convincingly argue for its modification, as they speak from experience and commitment.

In essence, the effectiveness of cross-generational leadership hinges on leaders' willingness to practice what they preach. By doing so, they pave the way for genuine dialogue, mutual respect, and meaningful change within the organization.

There's no one-size-fits-all approach to managing across generations. However, the approach that works best is maintaining openness and striving to understand each generation's perspective. The solution lies in maintaining openness and striving to understand the unique perspectives of each generation. This doesn't have to be a secretive process. Discussing these generational differences with your team can further awareness, which is instrumental in supporting change and achieving balance. A potential activity could be to gather your employees and encourage them each to bring an example of what they genuinely admire about another generation, along with something they wish to understand better about a different generation.

Activity for Generational Understanding and Respect:

Purpose: To develop mutual respect, understanding, and collaboration among employees from different generations by sharing positive perceptions and areas of curiosity about each other.

Materials Needed:

- Comfortable seating arrangement for a group discussion
- Whiteboard or large paper for note-taking
- Markers or pens
- Optional: Refreshments to create a relaxed atmosphere

Steps:

1. **Introduction (10 minutes):**
    - Begin by explaining the purpose of the activity: to enhance mutual respect and understanding across generations within the team.

- Emphasize that the goal is to share what they admire about other generations and express curiosity about aspects they wish to understand better.

2. **Individual Reflection (10 minutes):**
    - Ask each participant to take a few minutes to reflect and write down two points:
        - One thing they genuinely admire about another generation in the workplace.
        - One thing they are curious about or wish to understand better regarding another generation.

3. **Sharing in Pairs (15 minutes):**
    - Have participants pair up with someone from a different generation.
    - Each person takes turns sharing their points with their partner.
    - Encourage active listening and respectful dialogue during this exchange.

4. **Group Discussion (30 minutes):**
    - Reconvene as a whole group.
    - Invite volunteers to share highlights from their pair discussions.
    - On the whiteboard, create two columns labeled "Admire" and "Curiosity."
    - Record the shared points in the respective columns.

5. **Facilitated Discussion (20 minutes):**
    - Lead a group discussion based on the points recorded on the whiteboard.
    - Explore common themes and differences.
    - Encourage participants to ask questions and seek further insights from their colleagues.

6. **Action Planning (15 minutes):**
    - Discuss how the insights gained can be applied to improve team dynamics and work processes.
    - Identify specific actions or initiatives the team can undertake to address areas of curiosity and build on admired traits.

7. **Wrap-Up (10 minutes):**
    - Summarize the key takeaways from the activity.
    - Thank participants for their openness and contributions.
    - Highlight the importance of ongoing dialogue and continuous improvement in fostering an inclusive workplace.

Follow-Up:

- Schedule regular check-ins to discuss progress and revisit any ongoing questions or new insights that arise.
- Encourage continued sharing of positive observations and curiosities in team meetings or through internal communication channels.

Dynamic Shifts: Embracing a Cross-Generational Workforce

The evolution of our professional atmosphere has been significantly influenced by the increasing presence of a cross-generational workforce. The diversity of age groups brings a wealth of perspectives and experiences, which, if managed effectively, can drive innovation and growth. However, to fully harness the potential of this diverse workforce, it's crucial to examine and refine our approaches to followership, leadership, and workplace culture. Here are some key considerations and questions to explore:

Embracing Flexible Policies

Flexible policies are not just perks but vital components of a modern workplace. They can revolutionize work-life balance and productivity by accommodating the varying needs of different generations. For instance:

- **Younger Employees** might value remote work options and flexible hours that allow them to pursue personal projects or further education.
- **Middle-aged Workers** often need flexibility to manage family responsibilities.
- **Older Employees** may appreciate phased retirement plans or opportunities to mentor younger colleagues.

Question: How can embracing flexible policies truly revolutionize our approach to work-life balance and productivity?

Valuing Every Team Member

A workplace where every team member feels genuinely valued and heard is one where innovation thrives. This involves not only listening to different perspectives but also acting on them. Imagine a workplace where:

- **Young professionals** feel confident in proposing new ideas.
- **Experienced employees** have their knowledge and wisdom recognized and utilized.

Question: What would our workplace look like if every team member felt genuinely valued and heard?

Practicing Inclusive Culture

Promoting an inclusive culture goes beyond policies; it requires genuine commitment. Regularly assessing our practices and seeking feedback can reveal gaps between our inclusive aspirations and reality.

Question: Can we honestly say we practice the inclusive culture we promote, or are there gaps we need to address?

Celebrating Generational Contributions

Fully embracing and celebrating the unique contributions of each generation can transform team dynamics. A multigenerational team that leverages the strengths of all members can:

- **Younger employees** bring fresh perspectives and tech-savviness.
- **Older employees** offer deep industry knowledge and mentorship.

Question: How might our team dynamics change if we fully embraced and celebrated the unique contributions of each generation?

Leadership by Example

Leaders play a pivotal role in setting the tone for the entire organization. They must embody the values of respect, inclusivity, and collaboration. When leaders actively demonstrate these values, they inspire their teams to follow suit.

Question: Are our leaders setting the right example by adhering to the practices and values we stand for?

Unlocking Potential through Dialogue

Open dialogue across generational lines can uncover untapped potential. Creating spaces for these conversations can lead to greater understanding and collaboration.

Question: What untapped potential could we unlock by fostering more open dialogue across generational lines?

Aligning Actions with Words

Ensuring that our actions align with our words is crucial for maintaining trust and integrity. This means consistently applying our stated values in every aspect of our operations.

Question: How can we ensure that our actions align with our words when it comes to promoting respect and collaboration among all age groups?

Bridging the Generational Divide

Creating a cohesive and innovative team environment requires bridging the generational divide. This can involve:

- **Intergenerational mentorship programs** where knowledge flows both ways.
- **Collaborative projects** that leverage the diverse strengths of all team members.

Question: In what ways can we bridge the generational divide to create a more cohesive and innovative team environment?

By addressing these questions and focusing on the unique strengths of a cross-generational workforce, organizations can create a dynamic and inclusive professional atmosphere that fosters growth, innovation, and mutual respect.

Additional Activities for Navigating the Cross-Generational Workforce:

These exercises can be conducted individually or within team meetings.

1. **Generational Value Mapping:**
   - Create a chart with a section for each generation in your team. Ask team members from each generation to list what they value most in their work. Then, discuss how these values can complement each other, supporting a more cohesive team dynamic. Ask team members to identify where they see common ground and capitalize on what the team shares to move forward together.

2. **Communication Style Workshop:**

- Hold a workshop where team members present their preferred communication tools and styles, explaining why they find them compelling. This exercise can lead to a deeper understanding among team members and the development of a hybrid communication strategy that respects everyone's preferences. You and a strong co-leader should be present first to set the tone. Ask for bravery among your team for this experience.

Preparing for Future Generational Shifts:

As we look to the future, it's clear that the workplace will continue to evolve. Leaders must stay informed about emerging trends and how they might influence generational dynamics. For instance, the rise of artificial intelligence and remote work will likely shape all generations' expectations and working styles.

Leaders should cultivate a culture of continuous learning and flexibility to prepare for these shifts. Encourage team members to engage with new technologies, regardless of their generational affiliation. Additionally, creating a culture of mentorship and lifelong learning can help ensure your workforce is prepared for the changes to come.

Remember, as a leader, you play a pivotal role in establishing the workplace atmosphere. When team members of all generations adopt new technologies, welcoming these changes is essential. Resistance to new ideas can alienate employees, driving them to seek employment elsewhere, in places more receptive to innovative technologies, methodologies, and perspectives. Embracing change not only demonstrates your adaptability but also encourages a culture of continuous improvement and learning.

Followership is about leveraging your leadership skills to support and nurture the ideas and concepts of those you lead. It means recognizing the value of diverse perspectives and encouraging contributions from everyone, regardless of their age or experience level. By actively listening and showing enthusiasm for new initiatives, you create an environment where all team members feel valued and empowered.

In doing so, you forge a collaborative and progressive work environment. This not only boosts morale and engagement but also drives the organization forward, ensuring it remains competitive in a rapidly evolving landscape. By championing innovation and demonstrating a commitment to growth, you set a positive example for your team, inspiring them to reach their full potential and contribute their best ideas.

Ultimately, effective leadership in a multigenerational workplace requires a balance of guiding and supporting. It involves creating an atmosphere where new technologies and methodologies are not just accepted but celebrated. By doing so, you build a resilient and forward-thinking team capable of navigating the challenges and opportunities of the modern workplace.

By implementing strategies that anticipate future trends, leaders can build resilient teams in the face of change and equip them to leverage new opportunities for innovation and growth. This forward-thinking approach ensures that your organization remains competitive and can attract talent from all generations, nurturing a dynamic work environment prepared to meet tomorrow's challenges.

Chapter 10: Bridging the Generational Gap

When I began my professional office career in the spring of 2010 as an Item Processing Specialist, typical leaders—directors, vice presidents, and chiefs—were seasoned professionals in their 40s, 50s or 60s. Fast forward to today, and I've witnessed a significant shift in what leadership looks like. Pivotal roles are now occupied by a diverse age range of professionals, including young leaders in their late 20s and early 30s.

Recent data indicates a notable increase in younger adults, particularly those in their 20s and 30s, holding higher management positions compared to previous decades. Several key factors contribute to this trend.

> First, the level of higher education attainment among young adults has risen significantly, providing them with the necessary qualifications for advanced roles. For instance, the share of young adults with bachelor's degrees has increased, enhancing their prospects in the job market (Pew Research Center).
>
> Second, labor market trends show a substantial rise in full-time employment among young adults. The percentage of 25 to 29-year-olds working full-time has grown from 65% in 1993 to 70% today, and from 68% to 73% for those aged 30 to 34 (*Pew Research Center*).
>
> Third, the phenomenon known as the Great Resignation has led to higher turnover in management positions, creating more opportunities for younger professionals to ascend to these roles (*Insight by FactSet*).

These trends highlight a positive shift towards younger adults assuming higher management roles, which is crucial for bridging the generational gap in the workforce. This change reflects a broader societal transformation in our perceptions of leadership.

> Personal Anecdote: At 22, I started my management journey as the youngest manager in a medium-sized bank's operations center. I faced the challenge of leading teams where every member was older and more experienced than I was. This pattern continued as I climbed the corporate ladder, becoming an Assistant Vice President at a small credit union at 26, a director at 28, and a Vice President at 31. I was often the youngest person in each of these roles, learning how to work with peers and superiors who were significantly older.

Did I always "act my age"? Not necessarily. Leadership in a diverse workplace requires adaptability. I found ways to connect with older colleagues by aligning with their generational mannerisms, while with peers closer to my age, I could adopt more comfortable connections.

A standard piece of advice is to be genuine and consistent in all interactions. While this holds true for honesty and transparency, finding common ground with people of different generations is critical to building connections.

When faced with remarks about my age or lack of experience with past events, I often respond with curiosity and openness. Whether discussing the Columbia space shuttle launch, Chernobyl, the fall of the Berlin Wall, Watergate, Three Mile Island, or the lowering of the voting age, I found that having a general knowledge of history was invaluable in social interactions.

But it's not just about memorizing dates. Understanding the significance of past events and how they've shaped the world helps in relating current events to experiences familiar to older generations. This understanding is crucial for young people learning about past generations and older generations understanding the significance of events for the newer generations.

I was born in 1990, meaning I've never known a world without the internet. This starkly contrasts with many of my colleagues who remember a time before the World Wide Web. Recognizing this difference in experiences is vital for effective collaboration across generations.

As my career developed, I grappled with self-doubt, questioning whether I was too young to handle the responsibilities I'd been given. I had to overcome those hurdles internally through the process of realizing that age is just a number. I learned to focus on my abilities and contributions, gradually earning respect and recognition for my work, not my age.

The evolution of my self-perception mirrors a more significant change in the workplace. The generational shift in leadership roles reflects a growing understanding that age does not necessarily correlate with leadership ability. The notion that the most senior person is the best-suited leader is an outdated bias. We are moving toward a culture where leadership is based on merit, skills, and the ability to inspire and guide, regardless of age.

However, addressing generational dynamics requires dealing with age-related stereotypes. Labeling people based on their age or generational group can be as harmful as other forms of discrimination. Recognizing and appreciating the unique strengths and perspectives each generation brings is essential. Younger leaders like myself often bring fresh ideas and innovative approaches, while more experienced colleagues contribute wisdom, stability, and a deep understanding of industry trends.

Instead of assigning labels, we can have a dialogue around generational differences that create an environment of mutual respect. Each generation—from Baby Boomers to Generation Z—has its own set of experiences and viewpoints, and this diversity enriches our workplaces and drives innovation.

The journey through different generational landscapes in leadership has taught me invaluable lessons, like the importance of viewing each individual as a unique contributor, not just a representative of their age group. As we navigate a multi-generational workforce, let us focus on the qualities that unite us: our shared goals, our collective wisdom, and our common pursuit of excellence. Doing so can create a more inclusive, dynamic, and productive work environment for all.

Harmful Self-Talk & Generational Discrimination

Throughout the early years of my career, I struggled to overcome the self-imposed hurdle of my age. Doing so took a conscious effort to shift my mindset.

For years, I constantly doubted that I should be in my role, primarily because of my age and the fact that others had significantly more experience than me. This self-doubt often manifested in subtle yet impactful ways. I would second-guess my decisions, leading to procrastination and missed opportunities. During meetings, I hesitated to voice my opinions, fearing they would be dismissed or deemed naïve. This hesitation not only undermined my confidence but also prevented me from fully showcasing my capabilities.

The negative outcomes were profound. My performance suffered as I frequently played it safe, avoiding taking risks that could have propelled my projects forward. My well-being took a hit as the constant stress and anxiety of not feeling "enough" led to burnout and a persistent feeling of inadequacy. Professionally, I was stagnating. While my peers were advancing, I felt stuck in a cycle of self-sabotage, unable to break free from my own limiting beliefs.

The turning point came when I decided to shift my mindset. I started by acknowledging my achievements and the unique perspectives I brought to the table, regardless of my age. I sought mentorship and feedback, allowing myself to grow from constructive criticism rather than be crippled by it. Gradually, I began to take small risks, which built my confidence incrementally.

The outcome of this mindset shift was transformative. My performance improved as I became more decisive and proactive. My well-being flourished as I felt more at ease and self-assured in my role. Professionally, I began to gain recognition and new opportunities for advancement. By embracing my value and contributions, I was able to break free from the cycle of self-doubt and truly thrive in my career.

Although similar self-inflicted thoughts resurface occasionally, I've learned that age is just a number, and people are beginning to appreciate me for who I am, including my youthfulness.

In all seriousness, I've learned not to let my age define me or limit my potential. Despite the occasional negative comment or feeling excluded from conversations about the '80s and '90s, I've realized that my age is irrelevant to my performance.

This shift in perspective has helped me overcome internal doubts, a challenge faced by many young professionals I meet and converse with. My self-doubt had previously cast a long shadow over my career. There were instances when my contributions were overshadowed by older colleagues, and I couldn't help but feel that my ideas were dismissed because of my age. This subtle age-related discrimination exacerbated my insecurities, making me question my place in the professional world even more.

The impact of this self-doubt was multifaceted. I often found myself over-preparing for presentations to compensate for my perceived lack of experience, which led to unnecessary stress and exhaustion. I would defer to more seasoned colleagues in discussions, inadvertently reinforcing the notion that my insights were less valuable. This not only affected my performance but also stunted my professional growth, as I missed out on opportunities to demonstrate leadership and innovation.

However, since shifting my mindset, the transformation has been remarkable. I now approach my role with a sense of confidence and clarity. Embracing my unique perspective and the fresh ideas I bring to the table has allowed me to contribute more effectively and assertively. The change has also influenced how others perceive me; colleagues now seek my input and value my contributions, recognizing the strengths I bring to the team.

This newfound confidence has positively impacted my well-being. I am no longer weighed down by the constant need to prove myself due to my age. Instead, I focus on continuous learning and growth, which has led to a more fulfilling and balanced professional life. By overcoming my internal doubts, I've set a precedent for other young professionals, demonstrating that age does not define one's capability or potential. The journey has been empowering, turning what was once a source of insecurity into a foundation for resilience and success.

Age discrimination is a two-way street. Instead of judging someone as too young or lacking the "right" number of years of experience, we should evaluate their work ethic, ability to answer complex questions, independent thinking, creativity, and empathy. These qualities are far more indicative of a person's potential and capability than the mere number of years they have been in the workforce.

Generational discrimination, though not as commonly discussed, is equally prevalent and harmful. It's similar yet distinct from age discrimination. How often have we heard sweeping statements about 'Millennials' or 'Gen Zs'? These labels unfairly segregate entire groups under a single stereotype, ignoring the diversity of skills and perspectives within each generation, and each individual. Such generalizations can lead to biased decisions that overlook individual talent and potential.

We should hire the person, not the generational stereotype. In my career, I was fortunate to have those who looked beyond my age and generational trends, which don't often apply to me. They saw my unique contributions and potential rather than fitting me into a preconceived mold. If you ask them now, they'll affirm that hiring me was a positive choice. Was I different? Yes. Did I bring a new approach or mindset? Absolutely. And it was precisely what the organization needed to move forward.

This experience taught me that when we focus on individual strengths and qualities, rather than age or generational labels, we unlock the true potential of our workforce. Embracing diversity in thought, experience, and background enriches an organization and drives innovation. It's time we moved beyond stereotypes and recognized the value that each person brings, irrespective of their age or generational affiliation.

Technology – The Generational Gap (or is it?)

It's clear that the technological transformation from the pre-1990s to the present has deeply influenced generational dynamics. Initially, computers were intimidating machines reserved for business or academic purposes, with limited personal interaction. This scenario shifted dramatically after the 1990s, as personal computers became ubiquitous, bringing with them a need for operating systems, word processing, spreadsheets, and internet browsing skills.

Once a novel concept, the internet has become an integral part of life for the post-1990s generations, encompassing everything from email and search engines to online shopping and social media. Similarly, mobile technology's journey from a rare luxury to a necessity, evolving from basic cell phones to sophisticated smartphones with various features, reflects this generational shift.

Social interactions, too, have been reshaped. Where once conversations happened in person, over the phone, or through letters, they now take place over email and the advent of social media platforms like Facebook, Twitter, and LinkedIn transformed how we connect and share information. Entertainment has undergone a similar revolution; the pre-1990s era relied on radio, TV, and cinema, and the digital age brought about an era of video games, online streaming, and diverse digital content.

Attitudes toward technology have also evolved. The initial awe and skepticism, a blend of excitement about new inventions and apprehension regarding the rapid changes they brought, gradually transitioned to a more universal acceptance.

Crucially, adaptability to technological changes has been a defining feature of these generational shifts. This stark difference in technological adaptation underscores the profound impact of digital literacy on our society, illustrating how it has become a pivotal factor in the generational divide.

In addition to the technologically driven generational divide, we see a growing trend of younger leaders taking on leadership roles, with more followers from senior generations. This dynamic presents unique challenges and opportunities that are worth exploring. Younger leaders may bring fresh perspectives and innovative approaches, while older followers offer invaluable experience and wisdom. However, this age difference can also lead to potential pitfalls, such as differing communication styles, resistance to change, and preconceived notions about authority and expertise.

Navigating these challenges requires mutual respect and understanding. Younger leaders can benefit from actively seeking the insights and experiences of their seasoned team members, fostering an environment of collaboration rather than hierarchy. They should also strive to demonstrate their competence and leadership skills, earning the trust and confidence of their older followers. On the other hand, older followers can contribute by being open to new ideas and methods, leveraging their experience to support and mentor younger leaders rather than viewing them as competition.

Creating positive outcomes in such a dynamic involves clear and open communication, empathy, and a willingness to learn from one another. Establishing common goals and emphasizing the strengths each generation brings to the table can help bridge the gap and create a cohesive, productive team. By addressing these aspects, organizations can harness the full potential of a diverse, multigenerational workforce.

It's Not Just About the Younger Generations

I love the seasoned generations' valuable contributions to the workplace. Their presence is not just a nod to diversity but offers organizations a strategic advantage. Seasoned employees have a wealth of experience, often spanning decades; they are reservoirs of wisdom and insight. The depth of knowledge garnered through various industry cycles offers a rich perspective, particularly when navigating complex business landscapes.

I've observed the steadfast work ethic and reliability that seasoned colleagues bring. Their dedication is a testament to their professional upbringing, which often sets a positive example for younger team members. Work ethic is about more than showing up; it's about consistency in quality and a dedication to excellence that can inspire an entire team.

Another aspect that stands out is interpersonal skills. Years of professional interactions and diverse team experiences have honed older workers' ability to communicate, mentor, and provide constructive feedback. Interpersonal skills are crucial in building a cohesive team environment and encouraging a culture of growth. Stability and maturity can also bring a sense of balance to the workplace. Maturity is more than age; it comes from living a life, gathering experiences, and learning lessons, contributing to a more grounded approach to business challenges and team dynamics. A diversity of perspectives is crucial, and older employees add a rich layer to the discussion. Their viewpoints often challenge prevailing trends and group thinking, offering a broader, more comprehensive understanding.

More experienced employees' professional networks can be a goldmine for business development, mentorship, and industry insight. These networks are relationships forged and nurtured over time, often leading to opportunities beyond the immediate scope of work. Seasoned employees know how to build relationships without social media—that's all they had before the 2000s. Being connected on LinkedIn is like Facebook; you could have hundreds of connections, but who can you count on? You can rely on the people with whom you forged deep, face-to-face relationships. Seasoned professionals know how to start, maintain, and grow powerful business relationships.

Interestingly, I've consistently noticed a lower turnover rate among more mature colleagues. Recent research indicates a growing trend of older adults remaining in their jobs and with their current companies. The U.S. Bureau of Labor Statistics reports that the labor force participation rate for people aged 65 and older has been increasing over the past few decades. This trend is supported by findings from the Employee Benefit Research Institute, which show that many workers plan to work beyond the traditional retirement age of 65.

Employers are recognizing the value of experienced older workers and are implementing strategies to retain them, such as offering flexible work arrangements, part-time positions, and phased retirement programs, as highlighted by AARP. Furthermore, the Society for Human Resource Management (SHRM) notes that older employees tend to have lower turnover rates compared to their younger counterparts, often due to higher levels of job satisfaction and loyalty.

Advances in healthcare and an increased focus on healthy lifestyles are also contributing factors, allowing older adults to remain physically and mentally capable of working longer, according to the National Institute on Aging. Additionally, economic factors such as the need to supplement retirement savings and the impact of economic downturns on retirement plans have led many older adults to continue working, as detailed by the Center for Retirement Research at Boston College.

These factors collectively illustrate a significant shift in the workforce, with older adults staying active in their careers and contributing valuable experience and stability to their organizations.

Stability In Multigenerational Teams

Employee stability helps maintain a consistent work environment and reduces the costs associated with frequent hiring. Beyond professional understanding, the life experiences seasoned generations bring often enrich the workplace culture the most. Extensive workplace experiences foster attributes like empathy, patience, and a deeper understanding of human dynamics—indispensable qualities in any professional setting.

Contrary to popular belief, many older workers I've encountered are enthusiastic about learning new technologies. They often bring a unique approach to these new tools, blending their foundational knowledge with a willingness to evolve. Research by the American Association of Retired Persons (AARP) highlights that older workers are increasingly engaging with new technologies and digital tools, driven by both professional and personal motivations (AARP, "The Business Case for Workers Age 50+: A Look at the Value of Experience 2015").

Additionally, a study published in the "Journal of Occupational and Organizational Psychology" found that older employees often exhibit a strong commitment to lifelong learning and adaptability, which enhances their ability to integrate new technologies into their work (Kooij, T. A. M. "The influence of future time perspective on work engagement and job performance: The role of job crafting").

Moreover, the World Economic Forum reports that older workers are not only willing to learn new technologies but also often excel in leveraging these tools to improve productivity and innovation, thanks to their extensive experience and problem-solving skills (World Economic Forum, "How to reskill and retrain older workers").

These insights counter the stereotype of older workers being resistant to technological change and demonstrate their valuable contribution to modern, tech-driven workplaces.

The older generations excel in leadership and mentoring roles, often stepping into these positions naturally. Their guidance imparts knowledge and nurtures the next generation of professionals, creating an enduring legacy of skills. Our seasoned generation is a pillar of wisdom, stability, and depth. Their contributions go beyond mere experience, adding insight, strength, and richness to the workplace, proving that their presence is invaluable in the ever-evolving tapestry of the modern professional world.

Closing the Gap

We must not be divided by generational gaps but become the bridge that links us all together.

The issue of being trapped in our smartphones is now an all-generational one, not just confined to the younger population. Everyone, from teens to seniors, finds themselves drawn into the digital world, affecting our daily lives and interpersonal relationships. Similarly, a world of high interest rates isn't just a problem the older generations faced; it's impacting all of us now, affecting mortgages, loans, and savings alike. These challenges highlight more similarities that unite us than divide us.

I believe you'll find that generational differences are less about impending mistakes and more about evolution. Aren't the younger generations a product of the previous ones? For the young generations reading this, remember how it felt to be placed in a generational mold. Keep that in mind when Gen Z, Gen Alpha, and whatever generations come next begin to enter the realms of leadership and followership.

Instead of focusing on what separates us, let's celebrate the common experiences we share. Each generation has faced its own set of challenges and has adapted in unique ways. By recognizing these shared struggles and supporting each other, we can create a more cohesive and understanding society. Whether through mentorship programs, collaborative projects, or simply by listening to each other's stories, we can build bridges across the generational divide.

Please, let's stop the generational shaming. You'll never hear me say, "Well, they're a Baby Boomer, so that explains it." Refrain from pigeonholing younger workers with comments like, "Well, he's a Millennial, so he doesn't understand." Imagine these phrases were about gender, race, religion, or sexual orientation. They would not stand, nor should they. Be more aware of generational bias and combat its influence on our decisions.

Regardless of your generation, and whether you're a leader or a follower, take the message of this chapter and live it forward. As we urge people not to discriminate based on gender, sexual preference, age, and other demographics, I ask you to perceive individuals based on their character, rather than the assumptions that might be made due to generational appearance.

Diversifying Perspectives

Incorporating Employee Voices Across Generations: To truly bridge the generational gap, we must understand and integrate the perspectives of employees from various age groups. Initiatives like intergenerational focus groups and mentorship programs can facilitate open dialogues, allowing each generation to share their work experiences, expectations, and visions for the future. Documenting these discussions and sharing outcomes across the organization enables leaders to advance a culture of inclusivity and mutual respect.

Empirical Evidence on Generational Dynamics: Recent studies have shed light on how different generations perceive work-life balance, career progression, and workplace culture. The Pew

Research Center highlights varying attitudes toward technology, authority, and job loyalty among Baby Boomers, Gen Xers, Millennials, and Gen Zers. Baby Boomers generally show a cautious but appreciative approach to technology, often valuing its utility but wary of its overuse. They tend to respect traditional authority structures and exhibit strong job loyalty, often staying with one employer for many years. Gen Xers are characterized by their adaptability to technology, having witnessed its rapid evolution. They display a balanced view on authority, valuing both independence and structure, and tend to be moderately loyal to their jobs, often seeking work-life balance. Millennials are typically tech-savvy, embracing new technologies with enthusiasm. They often question traditional authority, preferring a more collaborative and inclusive approach. Job loyalty among Millennials is lower, with many seeking purpose and fulfillment in their careers, leading to more frequent job changes. Gen Zers are digital natives, fully integrated with technology from a young age. They challenge authority and prefer fluid, less hierarchical structures. Job loyalty for Gen Zers is the lowest among the generations, as they prioritize flexibility, innovation, and personal growth in their career choices. Incorporating these findings into leadership strategies can help tailor approaches to meet each generational cohort's unique needs, enhancing job satisfaction.

Leveraging Technology to Bridge the Gap: Leaders can tailor training programs based on varying comfort levels with digital tools, ensuring that all employees, regardless of age, have the skills to excel in their roles. Creating opportunities for cross-generational collaboration on technology-driven projects can promote knowledge exchange. For example, pairing a tech-savvy Gen Z employee with a Baby Boomer with extensive industry experience on a digital transformation project can yield new insights that neither could achieve alone.

Leaders who focus on these areas of enhancement can better navigate the challenges of heading up a multi-generational workforce, creating a more dynamic, inclusive, and productive work environment that leverages each generation's strengths.

Conclusion

The journey through the evolving landscape of cross-generational leadership is both a challenge and an opportunity. This chapter's reflections illuminate the path toward a more inclusive and adaptable leadership model.

We must embrace the diversity that different generations bring to the workplace, not as a divide but as a mosaic of experiences, perspectives, and skills that can enhance our collective endeavors. Integrating the voices of cross-generational employees acknowledges each group's unique contributions and needs, encouraging an environment where everyone feels valued.

Ongoing workforce research offers a solid foundation for these discussions, providing evidence-based insights into changing workforce dynamics. Research, coupled with visual aids, can offer clarity regarding generational differences, making information accessible to leaders and employees alike.

Furthermore, the strategies outlined for addressing technological gaps highlight the pivotal role of continuous learning in bridging the generational divide. Leaders who leverage technology as a common ground and collaboration tool build bridges between different age groups, facilitating knowledge exchange that benefits the entire organization.

I call on leaders to lead with empathy, openness, and a commitment to understanding each generation's unique strengths and challenges. Doing so enables us to transcend stereotypes, forging a workplace culture that celebrates diversity, encourages mutual respect, and leverages all generations' collective wisdom. As we move forward, let us remember that the true strength of our organizations lies in our ability to unite diverse talents toward a common purpose.

Remember, leaders lead from the front. Be bold in bridging the general gaps and breaking down preconceived divides.

Chapter 11: The Difficult Talk (Followership)

Having difficult discussions and making tough decisions is part of wearing the leadership hat. These moments often define a leader's ability to steer their team or organization through turbulent times. However, in the midst of focusing on leadership, we often fail to acknowledge followership in these challenging conversations. The role of a follower is crucial, yet it tends to be overlooked. In many cases, the followership role is just as important—if not more important—than the leadership role. A skilled follower can influence outcomes, provide critical support, and offer perspectives that leaders might miss. Recognizing this dynamic is key to developing a more collaborative and effective environment.

As we assume followership roles at whatever level we are in our career, having the courage to bring forth, navigate, and execute difficult discussions is part of the key dynamics. Effective followership requires a blend of assertiveness and diplomacy. Whether you are an entry-level intern needing to discuss how your current manager's communication style isn't clear, a mid-level manager tasked with delivering feedback to senior leadership, or a CEO having to tell the board of directors that the timing isn't right for their requested objectives, these conversations require careful preparation and tact.

For example, as an intern, approaching your manager about communication issues might involve documenting specific instances where misunderstandings occurred and suggesting ways to improve clarity. It's about framing the conversation positively and constructively, showing that your intention is to enhance team productivity and morale.

On the other end of the spectrum, a CEO might face the daunting task of informing the board of directors that the timing isn't right. This requires not only presenting a well-reasoned argument backed by data but also anticipating possible objections and preparing responses. It's about balancing honesty with optimism, demonstrating a clear vision for the future while acknowledging the current constraints.

To navigate these difficult discussions effectively, followers can employ several strategies:

1. **Active Listening:** Engage fully in conversations, demonstrating that you value others' opinions. This builds trust and opens the door for more meaningful dialogue.
2. **Emotional Intelligence:** Recognize and manage your emotions, as well as those of others. This helps in

responding appropriately to various situations and maintaining a calm and professional demeanor.

3. **Constructive Feedback:** When providing feedback, focus on specific behaviors and their impact, rather than personal attributes. This makes your feedback easier to accept and act upon.

4. **Preparation:** Before entering into a difficult discussion, gather relevant information and plan your key points. Anticipate possible reactions and prepare your responses.

5. **Assertiveness:** Communicate your needs and concerns clearly and confidently, without being aggressive. This shows respect for both your perspective and that of others.

By recognizing the importance of followership in difficult discussions and employing effective strategies, we can navigate these conversations with confidence and contribute meaningfully to the success of our teams and organizations.

If you take nothing else from this chapter, remember this: it is perfectly okay to be nervous when engaging in a difficult discussion. It's equally okay to express that nervousness to the other person. In fact, admitting your nerves is a powerful way to show humility and vulnerability. This sets the stage for a meaningful conversation by emphasizing that, while the discussion is challenging, it is also very important to you and that you care deeply about its impact on the other party.

As you navigate through this chapter, keep this key understanding in mind: showing vulnerability is not a weakness but a strategic strength in handling difficult discussions.

Initiating Difficult Discussions

Engaging in challenging conversations requires a blend of bravery and sensitivity. Courage is necessary to voice your thoughts, concerns, and suggestions, especially when they might not align with the views of your leaders or peers. This might mean addressing issues such as unclear communication, unrealistic expectations, or ethical concerns. Tact, on the other hand, involves presenting your points in a way that is respectful and constructive.

For instance, instead of bluntly stating that a manager's communication is ineffective, you might say, "I've noticed that sometimes there are misunderstandings about our tasks. Could we perhaps find a way to clarify our communication to ensure we're all on the same page?" This approach not only highlights the issue but also shows your willingness to find a collaborative solution.

The key is to prepare thoroughly, choose the right moment, and frame your conversation in a way that emphasizes mutual goals and respect. By doing so, you create a foundation for open dialogue and demonstrate that you are a proactive and thoughtful member of the team.

Tips for Successful Difficult Conversations

Courage: Preparing Yourself Emotionally

1. **Stay Calm:**
    - **Tip:** Don't rely on anger. Delaying difficult conversations can lead to stress buildup, resulting in explosive reactions. Such outbursts may get your words out but will dilute the importance of your message.
    - **Strategy:** Avoid venting to a coworker or exploding at your leadership in the heat of the moment—they will focus only on your reaction, not the issue you're hoping to address. If you feel like you're on the verge of losing control, consider contacting

your company's Employee Assistance Program or call a trusted relative or friend.

2. **Practice:**

    o **Tip:** If you're not accustomed to having challenging discussions, practice is critical.

    o **Strategy:** Practice alone or role-play with a trusted friend. Record yourself articulating your concerns and review the footage to identify areas for improvement. If the topic is emotionally charged, use the recording to express those intense feelings first. This can help you approach the actual conversation with greater calm and perhaps even get a little chuckle out of the conversation.

3. **Engage Tactfully:**

    - **Tip:** Approach the conversation with respect and constructive intent.

    - **Strategy:** Frame your concerns positively and constructively. Instead of bluntly stating issues, suggest improvements and focus on mutual goals. For example, say, "I've noticed that sometimes there are misunderstandings about our tasks. Could we perhaps find a way to clarify our communication to ensure we're all on the same page?"

4. **Avoid Over-Preparing:**

    o **Tip:** Preparation is essential, but over-preparing can lead to overthinking.

    o **Strategy:** Focus on expressing what you genuinely mean rather than obsessing over your wording. Be clear about your main points but remain flexible and open to dialogue.

Conducting Difficult Discussions

Starting the conversation on the right foot is critical. Acknowledge that the discussion might be challenging; this sets the right tone and prepares everyone for potentially tough topics. Ask if it's a good time to talk and allow them to postpone (for no more than 24 hours). Once the stage is set, take a moment to compose yourself and communicate that the topic is complex for you. Showing vulnerability can foster empathy and signal that your message is important.

Avoid The Word Dump:

Once you start talking, it can be hard to stop. I've been guilty of this—once I begin, my thoughts and grievances pour out, causing me to lose sight of my original objective. This lack of control can lead to several negative outcomes:

1. **Dilution of Your Core Message:**

    o When you allow your grievances to flow unchecked, your main point can become lost in a sea of complaints. This dilutes the impact of your original message and makes it harder for the listener to understand and address your primary concern.

2. **Emotional Overload:**

    o Uncontrolled venting can lead to an emotional overload for both you and the listener. Expressing too many issues at once can overwhelm the other party, causing them to shut down or become defensive. This emotional flood can also leave you feeling drained and less able to handle the conversation effectively.

3. **Perceived Unprofessionalism:**
   - Rambling on about multiple issues can come across as unprofessional. It might make you seem unorganized or overly emotional, which can undermine your credibility and the seriousness of your concerns. Maintaining a focused and composed demeanor is crucial for being taken seriously.

4. **Escalation of Conflict:**
   - When grievances pour out uncontrollably, the conversation can quickly escalate into a conflict. The listener may feel attacked or criticized, prompting a defensive reaction that can lead to a heated argument rather than a constructive discussion.

5. **Loss of Empathy and Understanding:**
   - A barrage of complaints can make it difficult for the other party to empathize with your situation. They may feel bombarded and less inclined to see your perspective, reducing the likelihood of a positive outcome. Maintaining focus helps preserve mutual respect and understanding.

6. **Ineffective Problem-Solving:**
   - Venting too many issues at once prevents a clear focus on solving any one problem effectively. It scatters attention and resources, making it harder to find actionable solutions. By sticking to your main point, you can work collaboratively toward a resolution.

How to Avoid These Negative Outcomes

To prevent these negative outcomes, consider the following strategies:

- **Stay Focused on Your Objective:**
    - Before the conversation, identify your primary goal and stick to it. Write down key points to keep yourself on track and avoid veering off into unrelated grievances. Is there a theme to all your concerns? If there a high priority?
- **Take Breaks if Needed:**
    - If you feel yourself becoming overwhelmed or straying from your main point, don't be afraid to pause. Taking a moment to collect your thoughts can help you regain focus and maintain maneuverability over the conversation.
- **Practice Mindfulness:**
    - Being mindful of your emotions and reactions during the conversation can help you stay calm and composed. Practice deep breathing or other calming techniques to keep your emotions in check.
- **Seek Feedback:**
    - After the conversation, seek feedback from a trusted colleague or mentor on how you handled the discussion. This can provide valuable insights and help you improve your approach for future difficult conversations.

Framework for Conducting the Discussion

- **Example Opening Statement:** "Thank you for taking the time to meet with me today. I want to mention upfront that this might be a difficult discussion, and I appreciate your patience. Is now a good time to talk?" (Pause) "This topic is challenging for me, and I've spent the last few days thinking it over to ensure I address it correctly. Feel free to stop me at any point for questions. I may occasionally steer the conversation, but please understand this is not meant as disrespect." (Pause)

- **Main Discussion Point:** "My concern is regarding [insert topic here]." [Keep this to one or two sentences. Brevity is critical to successful dialogue.] (Pause, and allow the message to sink in)

Observe body language during and after your opening statement. How someone reacts can give you insights into their initial reactions and thoughts.

Indicators That They May Already Be Aware of Your Concern:

- Nodding in agreement before you've finished speaking.
- Offering preemptive responses or solutions.
- Smirking or frowning in a way that seems to anticipate what you're saying.
- Mirroring your emotions in a way that feels unnatural.
- Frequently touching their face or showing general signs of discomfort.

Signs That This Information Might Be New to Them:

- Tilting their head, indicating curiosity or the need for clarification.
- Leaning forward, showing engagement and interest in the discussion.
- Raising their eyebrows, signaling surprise or newfound understanding.
- Taking pauses to reflect, think, or formulate questions.
- Furrowing their brow, which can denote concentration or concern.

Once you've clearly expressed your concerns with supporting facts, the most difficult part of the conversation is over. As a follower, you can rely on the leader to decide the next steps. In my experience, the person you're speaking with often asks questions, leading to a natural discussion.

Closing the Discussion: Many people struggle with closing challenging discussions. Leaders might ask for suggestions or what action you'd like to see. Be prepared with a potential solution or next steps.

For example: "Thank you for hearing me out. Regarding the next steps, I suggest [insert suggestion here]./I feel that a follow-up with Person A and Person B is needed. Should I schedule that?"

Follow-Up: Your approach after the meeting depends on your relationship with the leader. Ideally, the leader will drive the discussion toward action items or a follow-up. However, if you feel directionless following the discussion, consider sending a follow-up email. Tailor the message to your leader and set up a follow-up meeting if necessary. See below for a sample email.

"Dear Mike,

I sincerely appreciate your willingness to discuss the issue of high water levels in our toilets today. It was a valuable opportunity for open and honest dialogue. Should any questions arise from our discussion or if you feel certain aspects were not thoroughly explained, please don't hesitate to reach out. I'm more than willing to provide further clarification or answer any questions. What would be your preferred course of action regarding the following steps? I am open to arranging another meeting or gathering more information as needed.

Sincerely,"

Depending on the issue, you may set up a follow-up in the first meeting. You may want to follow up in person or during your next one-on-one.

Receiving Difficult Discussions and Accepting the Outcome

This process is similar to the one above but approached with a somewhat reversed mentality. If asked whether it's a good time for a discussion, and it truly isn't, be honest about it. Briefly explain why, if appropriate, or if it's a personal issue, mention that and suggest a later time that day or the following morning to ensure you're in the right mindset. However, as a follower, you might not always have this option. If you become overly emotional, it's acceptable to politely request a pause in the meeting to manage these emotions, asking to reschedule for later that afternoon or the next day. In severe cases, you might not have a choice in the matter. Nonetheless, even requesting a short 10–15-minute break to compose yourself is reasonable and shows self-awareness.

Listening to what is being said can be the most challenging part of these conversations. If the difficult discussion revolves around you, you must remain calm, avoid interrupting, and not immediately become defensive. This is easier said than done, especially because our natural instinct is to defend ourselves when we hear information that doesn't portray us favorably.

No one wants to be seen as falling short of expectations or causing problems, but it's important to listen fully before responding. Maintain your composure. In some cases, you may be able to take a break or even leave for the day. Do whatever is needed to remain calm and keep the discussion productive.

If the topic concerns your performance, politely request documentation of this feedback and ask for time to review and respond.

In cases of performance-related discussions, it's likely your leader will have a document prepared with action items for improvement. Review this document carefully, ask questions for clarity, and ensure you fully understand the expectations.

Responding to Direct Questions: If you're asked a direct question that you're uncomfortable answering due to a lack of information, emotional compromise, or a belief that the leadership lacks full context, it's okay to speak up. You might respond with something like:

"Thank you for raising these concerns. I may not have all the necessary information to provide a proper response. May I have some time to review, prepare my thoughts, and then reconvene?"

Then, reflect on the events as you remember them. Avoid involving coworkers or speculating and stick to the facts as you understand them. If, during this review, you realize that you were in the wrong, the best course of action is to take responsibility.

A simple acknowledgment like "I take responsibility for that" is a start, but more can be done. Consider saying: "Thank you for bringing this to my attention. I accept full responsibility in this matter and propose the following solutions to address these issues. I'd be happy to outline these corrective actions in a document." This approach shows ownership of the problem and a willingness to correct it.

If you're unsure how to rectify the issues, don't hesitate to ask for help: "I appreciate the opportunity to correct my mistakes. However, I'm struggling with how to proceed. Could you provide resources or guidance to help me develop an action plan?"

Following Up on Corrective Actions: Finally, the most crucial part: whether you or your leadership created the action plan, you must follow up with your leader on your corrective actions. Regular updates, such as a weekly email or during one-on-one meetings, are essential. Waiting passively for your leader to address the issue is not advisable.

Addressing corrective steps proactively demonstrates respect and the seriousness with which you're treating the matter. Leaders are often more forgiving of those who make a concerted effort to rectify their mistakes than of those who do little and hope the issues fade away.

Accepting Outcomes as a Follower:

Accepting outcomes as a follower in difficult conversations requires a blend of grace, professionalism, and introspection. In the hierarchical structure of the workplace, recognizing the authority of leaders is crucial. It is important to respect their decisions, even if you find yourself at odds with them. This respect does not preclude you from expressing your thoughts; rather, it encourages a respectful and constructive exchange.

Navigating the emotional landscape of such conversations can be challenging. It's natural to experience strong feelings, especially when decisions impact you directly. Acknowledging these emotions privately allows you to manage them without disrupting the dialogue. If the intensity of your feelings threatens to overwhelm, requesting a short break to regain composure is both reasonable and wise.

Clarity often serves as a balm for discomfort. When outcomes are unclear or seem unjust, seeking further explanation can provide a more comprehensive understanding of the rationale behind decisions. Approach these inquiries with a genuine desire to understand rather than to challenge, fostering a more constructive interaction.

Adaptability stands as a testament to your professionalism. Embrace the changes that come with the decisions, whether they involve new responsibilities, performance enhancements, or shifts in your approach. Your willingness to adapt not only enhances your reputation but also reinforces your value as a resilient and reliable team member.

Professionalism must remain your guiding principle, regardless of the outcome. Expressing gratitude for the feedback and the opportunity to discuss the matter reflects maturity and a commitment to your role and the organization. This gratitude underscores your ability to maintain a positive and constructive attitude even in the face of challenging news.

Reflection is a critical component of accepting outcomes. Take the time to ponder the feedback and the decisions made. What lessons can you glean from this experience? How can you leverage this feedback for personal growth? This reflective practice enables you to set personal goals and develop a concrete plan for improvement, demonstrating your commitment to continuous development.

Following up with your leader is essential. Communicate your action plan and keep them informed of your progress. This proactive approach signals that you are not only taking the feedback seriously but are also dedicated to making the necessary changes. Regular updates help maintain transparency and show your leader that you are diligently working towards improvement.

Seeking support is not a sign of weakness but of wisdom. If you find yourself uncertain about how to proceed, don't hesitate to ask for additional training, mentorship, or resources. Leaders appreciate when team members seek the assistance needed to meet expectations effectively, highlighting your commitment to professional growth.

Ultimately, each difficult conversation and the subsequent acceptance of its outcomes serve to build resilience. These experiences are opportunities to grow, reinforcing your ability to navigate challenging situations with confidence and composure. Embracing these moments with an open mind and a willingness to learn transforms even the most challenging feedback into valuable opportunities for development.

Initiating and Responding to Difficult Conversations

Navigating Difficult Conversations

Start Point: Identify the need for a difficult conversation.
Decision Point 1: Is this conversation initiated by you or directed toward you?
- If initiated by you, proceed to "Preparing Your Points."
- If directed toward you, move to "Preparing to Listen."

Preparing Your Points:
- Briefly note key issues.
- Practice articulating your main concerns.
- Decide on a desired outcome.

Preparing to Listen:
- Open yourself to feedback.
- Prepare mentally to stay calm.
- Think of clarifying questions.

Initiating the Conversation:
- Check for a good time.
- Use an opening statement to set the tone.

Engaging in the Dialogue:
- Present your points clearly.
- Listen actively.
- Use pauses effectively.

Decision Point 2: Have you reached an understanding or need more time?
- If yes, proceed to "Closing the Discussion."
- If not, and more time is needed, schedule a follow-up meeting.

Closing the Discussion:
- Summarize agreed points.

- Thank the other party for their time.
- Plan for a follow-up.

Incorporating Diverse Scenarios: Examples for Multicultural and Remote Teams

Scenario 1: Navigating Cultural Differences in Difficult Conversations

- **Context:** You need to address a sensitive topic with a team member from a cultural background that avoids direct criticism.
- **Approach:** Begin by expressing appreciation for their work, then gently introduce your concern. Highlight common goals and use inclusive language to bridge cultural gaps.

Scenario 2: Addressing Issues in a Remote Team Setting

- **Context:** A misunderstanding has arisen within a remote team, leading to friction.
- **Approach:** Schedule a video call to ensure face-to-face interaction. Start with a personal check-in to build rapport before moving into the discussion. Use screen sharing to refer to specific examples, ensuring clarity.

Feedback Mechanisms: Encouraging Constructive Feedback from Leaders

Creating a Feedback-Inviting Environment:

- After presenting your points or listening to feedback, ask open-ended questions like, "How do you see us moving forward from here?" or "What can I do to improve or address this issue effectively?"
- Express your commitment to growth and improvement, making it clear you value their guidance and feedback.

- Schedule regular check-ins post-conversation to discuss progress and any ongoing support or adjustments needed.

The Lighter Side of Difficult Conversations

Navigating difficult conversations doesn't always have to be a solemn affair. Sometimes, a little humor can diffuse tension, build rapport, and make the whole experience less daunting. Here are some tips and tricks to bring a touch of light-heartedness to your serious discussions—without undermining the importance of the topics at hand.

1. **Break the Ice with Humor**
    - Starting a tough conversation can feel like stepping into a cold shower. Instead, try breaking the ice with a little humor to set a more relaxed tone.
    - **Example:** "Hey, I wanted to chat about something. Don't worry, it's not as bad as a surprise dentist appointment!"
2. **Use Relatable Comparisons**
    - Comparisons can make complex issues more relatable—and funny. They help illustrate your point while keeping the mood light.
    - **Example:** "Sometimes, our team meetings feel like trying to herd cats. Maybe we can brainstorm ways to add a bit more structure—without needing a litter box."
3. **Lighten the Mood with Exaggeration**
    - A bit of exaggerated humor can make your point in a memorable way. Just make sure it's clear you're joking.
    - **Example:** "I've noticed that our project timelines are more optimistic than a kid on Christmas Eve. Maybe we can dial back the enthusiasm just a smidge?"

4. **Self-Deprecating Humor**
    - Showing that you can laugh at yourself can put others at ease and create a sense of camaraderie.
    - **Example:** "I've had more misunderstandings about this new software than I'd like to admit. I thought 'cloud storage' meant we needed better weather conditions!"
5. **Comic Relief with Common Scenarios**
    - Acknowledging the awkwardness of a situation with a humorous twist can help everyone relax.
    - **Example:** "Remember that time we tried to have a meeting during a fire drill. - Let's aim for a more successful conversation this time around."

Practical Tips for Injecting Humor

Tip 1: Know Your Audience
- Not everyone appreciates the same type of humor. Gauge the other person's receptiveness to humor before diving in. A light joke is great, but a misjudged one can backfire.
- **Strategy:** If you're unsure, start with mild humor and see how it's received. Adjust accordingly based on their reaction.

Tip 2: Stay Professional
- Humor should enhance the conversation, not distract from it. Keep it professional and avoid jokes that could be misinterpreted or seen as inappropriate.
- **Strategy:** Stick to universally safe topics and avoid humor that targets individuals or sensitive subjects.

Tip 3: Timing is Everything

- Use humor at the right moments. A well-placed joke can relieve tension, but too much can undermine the seriousness of the discussion.
- **Strategy:** Use humor to start the conversation or to ease tension at tricky points, but always bring the focus back to the main issue.

Sample Dialogue with Humor

You: "Thanks for meeting with me today. I promise this won't be as painful as getting stuck in a three-hour meeting about parking policies."

Manager: (laughs) "I appreciate that. What's on your mind?"

You: "I've noticed that sometimes our project deadlines are a bit... shall we say, ambitious? Kind of like thinking we can run a marathon after a week of jogging."

Manager: "I see what you mean. What do you suggest?"

You: "Maybe we can set more realistic timelines, like aiming for a 5K before we tackle the marathon. It'll help keep us on track and less frazzled."

By incorporating humor into your difficult conversations, you can create a more positive and engaging atmosphere. Remember, the goal is to make the interaction smoother, more relatable, and ultimately, more effective. So go ahead, sprinkle in some humor and watch how it can transform a tough discussion into a constructive and even enjoyable experience.

Putting humor aside, there are situations and difficult discussions where humor has no place. For instance, when discussing someone's performance, time away from the office, medical or mental health issues, harassment, or other sensitive and important topics, humor should never be introduced. To use humor effectively, you must understand both your audience and the subject matter. If you're unsure, it's best to avoid humor altogether.

The Heart of Followership

Take a moment to reflect on your role within your team or organization. Consider the times when you've had to summon the courage to address difficult issues with your leaders or peers. How did those moments shape you? Did they make you feel more connected to your purpose, or did they leave you questioning your place?

As followers, we often underestimate the power we hold. Our voices can bring about significant change, inspire new directions, and correct courses that have gone astray. Yet, it requires a deep sense of self-awareness and bravery to speak up, especially when the stakes are high.

Think about a time when you felt frustrated by a lack of accountability or transparency. How did that affect your motivation and your view of leadership? Now, consider the impact you could have by addressing such issues constructively. By embracing your role as a follower, you are not just supporting your team but also shaping the culture of your organization. Your willingness to engage in difficult conversations can be a beacon of integrity and a catalyst for positive change.

Followers are often seen as the backbone of any organization, silently carrying the weight of collective efforts and progress. However, this role is much more dynamic and influential than it might appear. The power of followership lies in its potential to drive change from within, to challenge the status quo, and to foster an environment where accountability and transparency thrive.

Imagine a scenario where a follower steps up to address a pervasive issue, such as a lack of clear communication within the team. By voicing concerns and suggesting improvements, this individual not only enhances the workflow but also sets a precedent for openness and dialogue. This act of courage can ripple through the organization, encouraging others to share their insights and foster a culture of continuous improvement.

Followers who actively participate in difficult conversations demonstrate a commitment to the organization's values and goals. They embody the principle that leadership is not confined to titles or positions but is an intrinsic quality that can manifest at any level. Their actions show that everyone has a role in steering the organization toward success.

In moments of challenge, followers who rise to the occasion help build a resilient and adaptive team. They remind us that true followership is not about passive compliance but about active engagement and thoughtful contribution. By nurturing these qualities, followers transform themselves into influential leaders, paving the way for a more inclusive and dynamic organizational culture.

So, take pride in your role as the follower. Recognize the impact you can make and the importance of your voice. Embrace the opportunities to contribute meaningfully, knowing that your efforts are essential to the health and growth of your team and organization.

Finally

The art of navigating challenging conversations is not just a leadership skill but a critical component of effective followership. The courage to initiate, the grace to engage, and the wisdom to accept the outcomes of these conversations are foundational to personal and professional growth. Employing the strategies in this chapter—from preparing and initiating to listening and responding—equips us with the tools to handle difficult discussions with tact, empathy, and resilience.

This chapter offers practical tips and underscores the importance of emotional intelligence, the value of preparation, and the power of vulnerability in encouraging meaningful dialogue. Whether through direct conversations, leveraging technology for remote teams, or navigating cultural differences, the ability to engage in and learn from difficult discussions is pivotal.

By incorporating visual aids, embracing diverse scenarios, and establishing feedback mechanisms, we enhance our capacity to communicate effectively across a spectrum of situations. These skills are invaluable, not only in our current roles but as we navigate the complexities of professional landscapes and personal relationships.

Difficult talks are opportunities for growth, improvement, and deeper connection. Embracing our role in these conversations with confidence and a commitment to continuous learning paves the way for a culture of transparency, respect, and mutual support within our organizations and beyond.

Chapter 12: The Difficult Talk (Leadership)

Leaders must understand the importance of making difficult decisions before we learn how to have challenging conversations. Decisions on strategy, projects, services, products, and other business matters are challenging, but what I want to address are the difficult choices around leading people. As a leader, the decisions you make during difficult talks with your followers can be your most significant accomplishments or your biggest failures.

If you are anything like me, then making difficult decisions—providing tough performance evaluations or discussions, demoting, and terminating—doesn't come easily. I never want to see others in pain, dealing with the loss of a job, or facing the embarrassment of having to tell their loved ones about a tough time at work, not to mention the self-reflection and hardship they might face.

Avoiding causing others pain is commendable, but not addressing problems because you dread the potential outcomes makes you an ineffective leader. Failing to address poor performance or personnel problems will bring down all the team members you are charged with leading. Avoiding difficult conversations can result in top performers leaving, team members feeling frustrated, departments not meeting company goals, and an overall failure on your part to fulfill the most basic tenet of leadership: being accountable and holding others accountable.

Have you ever been in a position or organization where you've observed long-term underperformance, poor leadership, bad decisions, improper communication, or other negative indicators? How did you feel? Seriously, put the book down for a moment and think about how it felt when others were not held accountable for constantly failing—and when there was nothing you could do about it.

I bet you felt frustrated, annoyed, and questioned why you were giving 150% when others seemed to skate by without doing anything at all. I bet you even considered polishing your resume!

All of these feelings—and more—are experienced by our employees when we fail to act or be transparent about our actions.

Too often, organizations make decisions that benefit the underperformer, like moving them into another position, with few or no consequences for prior failures. Avoiding accountability sends a dangerous message to everyone on your team.

Sometimes, you must even remove someone from their position, or even terminate them. It happens. It's happening somewhere in the world right now. While I hope you did everything you could to help them succeed, sometimes termination is the best decision you can make for the individual and for everyone else. Your team will benefit from seeing leadership ensuring accountability and acting when poor performance is evident.

I will skirt the Human Resources line, which my HR team will likely cringe at. However, I believe transparency is the cornerstone for good organizations and relationships to become great. In that spirit, we have to be transparent (while remaining appropriate) about why a person is being removed, terminated, or downgraded. Saving face for the individual helps no one. Put it out there, take the five minutes of embarrassment, and move on.

Do you realize how contagious the lack of appropriate action toward poor performers is?

If you look around your organization and see people meeting or barely meeting expectations, ask yourself: When did I or other leaders make decisions that created this learned behavior? Did you allow someone to continue underperforming in a role for an extended period, failing to meet goals, and furthering long-term issues to develop? Did you promote people to get them out of the way? Did you fail to terminate or demote when you should have? Your team notices these actions, and consciously or subconsciously, other employees will start to believe that this behavior is acceptable. "They won't fire me if I do the bare minimum or even slightly less."

So, if you look around and see that this lack of accountability has created a stagnant organization where you make minor improvements but never really move the needle, what should you do?

Look at the leadership. Change the leadership.

Be upfront about why you are changing leadership. Employees will respect you more for it. Your best and brightest will hope that positive change is happening; those meeting the organization's expectations may start adopting a more productive outlook. You have also, perhaps most importantly, alerted underperformers that change is coming.

Leadership Accountability and Embracing Difficult Discussions

A vital characteristic of a great leadership team is the ability to have difficult discussions while maintaining positive relationships. This positivity is evident when team members can leave a challenging meeting and genuinely inquire about each other's personal lives or seamlessly transition into the next meeting without lingering negativity.

For example, I should be able to walk into my peer vice president's office, close the door, and say, "I have concerns about one of your employees' performances. Frankly, I'm worried they're not being held accountable, and you, as their leader, may not be aware." Conversely, my peer vice presidents, or anyone for that matter, should feel comfortable coming into my office to discuss concerns about my direction on a project, communication style, general leadership, or any other issue. All of this should be done without feeling personally attacked, with the understanding that the initiating party is acting with noble intent.

When someone asked me about my ideal leadership dynamic, my response was straightforward: "I dream of being part of an organization where I can speak freely without constantly filtering my words or replaying conversations in my mind, worried about being misunderstood."

Defensiveness often indicates the avoidance of a problem. A good leader does not become defensive but listens and learns when another leader approaches them with possible concerns.

Navigating Difficult Discussions: Having a difficult conversation with one of your followers requires thoughtfulness and preparation. I find role-playing to be incredibly valuable for preparing to initiate a challenging conversation. On several occasions, I have partnered with various peers and my human resources team to role-play a difficult discussion.

One of the most important things you can do is create an environment where employees feel safe engaging in conversations—even when they're difficult. The talk will already be challenging, and they deserve empathy, respect, and care, whether the conversation is the first one or a final dismissal.

However, balancing personal feelings in a difficult discussion can be tricky. You must be able to deliver your message, provide documentation, create a corrective action and expectation plan, and move forward. Holding the line is crucial. Doing so doesn't mean you can't be empathetic, but you must express that empathy while avoiding further issues, confusion, lack of performance, or disengagement.

The best approach to a complex discussion is Direct Empathetic Communication, as early discussed.

Strategies for Empathetic Leadership

Here are some ways to show empathy without compromising your stance:

1. **Offer Time Off**: After delivering the news, consider giving them the rest of day off, particularly if they react angrily. End the discussion, ask them to leave for the day, and plan

to reconnect tomorrow. Assure them that their outburst won't be held against them. We're all human, and difficult news can sometimes be taken poorly. You may be unaware of what's happening in their personal life that could contribute to their reaction. It's better to end the conversation and reconnect later with cooler heads.

2. **Avoid Information Overload**: Sometimes, leaders' hand over a lengthy document during the discussion without giving their followers time to read, understand, and respond to the materials. While you might summarize it, the employee may try to read it and get fixated on a single point. I prefer to have the conversation, take notes, and provide the documentation afterward.

Addressing Chronic Underperformance

Scenario: A leader faces the challenge of addressing a long-term employee's chronic underperformance. Through a series of documented meetings, the leader provides specific feedback, sets clear expectations, and offers support for improvement.

Steps to Approach:

1. **Documentation and Initial Assessment**: Begin by documenting specific instances of underperformance. Gather data and feedback from multiple sources to get a comprehensive view of the employee's performance issues. Assess whether the underperformance is due to skill gaps, personal issues, or lack of motivation.

2. **First Meeting**: Schedule a private meeting with the employee to discuss performance issues. Use specific examples to illustrate the problems. Approach the conversation with empathy, expressing your desire to help them improve. Clearly state the performance standards and expectations. Giving the employee time, 24 hours if

needed, to digest the information or respond. Scheduling a follow up meeting as needed.

3. **Creating an Improvement Plan**: Collaborate with the employee to develop a performance improvement plan. This plan should include clear, measurable goals, a timeline for achieving these goals, and the resources available to support the employee, such as training or mentoring.

4. **Regular Check-Ins**: Schedule regular check-in meetings to monitor progress. Use these meetings to provide constructive feedback, celebrate small successes, and address any ongoing challenges. Adjust the improvement plan as needed based on the employee's progress.

5. **Final Review**: At the end of the improvement period, conduct a final review meeting. If the employee has met the performance goals, acknowledge their hard work and discuss how they can continue to improve and contribute to the team. If they have not met the goals, discuss the next steps, which may include reassignment, further support, or termination.

Outcome: This approach demonstrates the importance of documentation, consistency, and fairness in managing underperformance. Clear expectations and regular feedback create a structured path for improvement. If the employee turns around their performance, it's a win for both the individual and the team. If not, fair and documented processes ensure that any necessary termination is handled with professionalism and respect.

By transparently navigating team restructuring and addressing chronic underperformance with empathy and structured plans, leaders can maintain trust, morale, and high performance within their teams. These real-world applications underscore the critical balance of empathy, accountability, and clear communication in effective leadership.

Feedback Mechanisms: Building a Feedback-Rich Culture

Developing a culture where feedback is an integral part of everyday operations is essential for the growth and success of any organization. A feedback-rich culture not only improves individual performance but also enhances team dynamics, encourages innovation, and drives continuous improvement. Here's an in-depth look at how to build and maintain such a culture through effective feedback mechanisms.

Creating a Feedback Loop

A robust feedback loop is the cornerstone of a feedback-rich culture. It ensures that feedback is not just given and received, but also acted upon, creating a continuous cycle of improvement and development.

Regular Check-Ins: Regular check-ins are structured, consistent meetings between team members and leaders. These sessions provide a dedicated time to discuss performance, address concerns, and set goals. To make the most of these check-ins:

- **Frequency and Consistency:** Schedule check-ins on a weekly or bi-weekly basis to maintain a steady flow of communication.

- **Clear Agenda:** Have a clear agenda for each meeting, focusing on both positive feedback and areas for improvement.

- **Two-Way Dialogue:** Encourage an open dialogue where both parties can share their perspectives and suggestions.

- **Actionable Outcomes:** Conclude each check-in with clear, actionable steps for both the team member and the leader.

Feedback Training: Feedback training is essential to equip both leaders and team members with the skills needed to give and receive feedback effectively. Effective feedback training should cover:

- **Constructive Feedback Techniques:** Teach how to give feedback that is specific, objective, and aimed at promoting growth.
- **Receiving Feedback:** Emphasize the importance of a growth mindset and being open to feedback without becoming defensive.
- **Role-Playing Exercises:** Conduct role-playing scenarios to practice giving and receiving feedback in a controlled environment.
- **Continuous Improvement:** Reinforce the idea that feedback is a tool for continuous improvement, not just a means of criticism.

Anonymous Feedback Channels: Anonymous feedback channels provide a safe space for team members to express their opinions and concerns without fear of retaliation. To establish effective anonymous feedback channels:

- **Digital Platforms:** Use digital tools and platforms that allow team members to submit feedback anonymously.
- **Regular Review:** Ensure that the feedback collected through these channels is reviewed regularly and taken seriously.

- **Transparency:** Communicate how anonymous feedback is being used to make improvements and decisions within the organization.
- **Encouragement:** Regularly remind team members of the availability of anonymous feedback channels and encourage their use.

Benefits of a Feedback-Rich Culture

Building a feedback-rich culture offers numerous benefits that extend beyond individual performance:

1. **Enhanced Communication:** Regular feedback fosters open communication, reducing misunderstandings and promoting a collaborative work environment.
2. **Improved Performance:** Constructive feedback helps individuals understand their strengths and areas for improvement, leading to better performance.
3. **Increased Engagement:** When team members see that their feedback is valued and acted upon, they are more likely to feel engaged and invested in their work.
4. **Innovation and Growth:** A culture of feedback encourages the sharing of ideas and perspectives, driving innovation and organizational growth.
5. **Stronger Relationships:** Regular, honest feedback helps build trust and stronger relationships among team members and leaders.

Implementing Feedback Mechanisms: Best Practices

To effectively implement feedback mechanisms, consider the following best practices:

- **Leadership Commitment:** Ensure that leaders are committed to fostering a feedback-rich culture and lead by example.
- **Cultural Integration:** Integrate feedback mechanisms into the organizational culture, making them a natural part of daily operations.
- **Feedback Diversity:** Encourage feedback from a diverse range of sources, including peers, subordinates, and external stakeholders.
- **Recognition and Rewards:** Recognize and reward team members who actively participate in and contribute to the feedback process.
- **Continuous Monitoring:** Continuously monitor and evaluate the effectiveness of feedback mechanisms, making adjustments as needed to improve their impact.

By creating a structured feedback loop, offering comprehensive feedback training, and establishing anonymous feedback channels, organizations can build a feedback-rich culture that promotes continuous improvement, innovation, and success.

Navigating Team Restructuring with Transparency

Scenario: A leader must navigate a team restructuring resulting in role changes and redundancies. The process involves transparently communicating the reasons for restructuring, the expected outcomes, and the support available to those affected.

Steps to Approach:

1. **Preparation**: Before announcing the restructuring, the leader should gather all relevant information and create a detailed plan outlining the reasons for the changes, the benefits for the organization, and the specific impacts on team members. Anticipate questions and concerns that employees might have.

2. **Initial Announcement**: Hold a team meeting to announce the restructuring. Begin with a clear explanation of why the restructuring is necessary, linking it to the organization's goals and future direction. Use straightforward language to ensure everyone understands the rationale behind the changes.

3. **Detailed Individual Conversations**: Schedule one-on-one meetings with each team member to discuss how the restructuring affects them personally. Be transparent about any role changes or redundancies. Clearly outline the support available, such as severance packages, job placement assistance, and counseling services.

4. **Continuous Communication**: Maintain an open line of communication throughout the transition period. Provide regular updates on the restructuring process and any additional support measures being implemented. Encourage team members to ask questions and express their concerns.

5. **Support Systems**: Implement support systems to help employees cope with the changes. This could include workshops on resume writing and interview skills, mental health support, and career counseling.

Outcome: By maintaining clear, compassionate communication, the leader can mitigate the negative impact of the restructuring on team morale and individual resilience. Transparency helps in maintaining trust, showing that the organization values its employees even in difficult times. This approach can lead to a smoother transition, with employees feeling more supported and understood.

The Soul of Leadership

As a leader, the decisions you make and the conversations you have with your team define the legacy you leave behind. These moments are not just about managing tasks or meeting goals; they are about touching lives and shaping futures.

Think back to a time when you had to make a tough decision regarding a team member. How did it feel? Did you struggle with the weight of your responsibility? Leadership is not just about the accolades and successes; it's also about the quiet, often painful moments when you must hold the line and make decisions that may hurt in the short term but are necessary for the long-term health of your team and organization.

Reflect on the leaders who have influenced you. What qualities did they possess that inspired trust and respect? How did they handle difficult conversations and decisions? Strive to embody those same qualities—empathy, fairness, transparency, and courage. Recognize that every difficult conversation is an opportunity to demonstrate your commitment to your team's well-being and to uphold the values you hold dear.

In these challenging moments, let your leadership be a source of strength and guidance. Show your team that you are willing to make the hard choices, not out of a desire for control, but out of a genuine care for their growth and the organization's success. Your actions, rooted in empathy and accountability, will set the tone for a culture of trust and high performance.

Finally

This chapter explored the importance of making tough decisions, holding difficult discussions, and holding accountability, particularly those involving the delicate task of leading people. As a leader, you will face challenges and emotional complexities when navigating these waters. Leadership action must be grounded in empathy, accountability, and transparency. Understanding and adapting to diverse cultural backgrounds demonstrates how you can maintain high performance and create a positive organizational culture even in the face of tough decisions.

Creating a feedback-rich culture serves as a reminder of the ongoing nature of leadership development. Taking a proactive approach to giving and receiving feedback will encourage growth and ensure you have fewer difficult conversations in the future.

This chapter is a roadmap to cultivating an effective and humane leadership style. By embracing the principles of direct, empathetic communication, cultural sensitivity, and feedback, you can navigate the most challenging aspects of your role with integrity and grace. This chapter calls on you to reflect on your practices, encouraging you to strive for a balance that respects the dignity of all involved while upholding the organization's standards. Through this balanced approach, you can inspire trust, encourage high performance, and build a workplace culture that is resilient, inclusive, and forward-looking.

Chapter 13: Leading Up: The Following Leader

Leading up is an art form that seems to be diminishing. Before I explain why (and show you what we can do about it), let's explore the concept of leading up and its benefits for leaders and followers.

"Leading up" happens when followers proactively attempt to have a positive influence on their leaders. Leading up is not about taking control or dictating to the leader. Instead, it's about helping your leaders understand the relationships between goals, tasks, and objectives so they can offer better direction. Better understanding ensures that your leader recognizes the importance of these elements and selects the appropriate priorities for the team.

The dynamic created by leading up expands outside the traditional confines of executing directives. Instead, leading up encourages followers to take the initiative to provide constructive feedback, propose innovative concepts, and assist leaders in understanding the impact of their choices.

At its core, leading up is anchored in a deep understanding of an organization's objectives and a commitment to its success. A follower who leads up must employ effective communication, mutual trust, and the courage to tactfully challenge those in senior positions. The ultimate goal of leading up is to make a meaningful contribution to the organization's success.

Why, then, is this practice diminishing? I believe the idea of leading up is sometimes misunderstood by those at all levels of their careers, and a better understanding would lead to wider adoption.

For example, my direct reports often challenge me when I take on tasks that are not appropriate for my position or leadership level. Recently, I assumed the role of project administrator. Why did I take on this role? Because I felt it was what the organization needed, and I often followed the philosophy that there is no task beneath me, no matter my rank or position. Well, you guessed it, one of my direct reports challenged me on this decision, noting that by taking on such a role, I might be hindering growth, accountability, and the long-term sustainability of the organization. After reflecting on my decision, I realized she was right. While I can still adhere to my mentality of never getting too big for my boots, I needed to reserve this approach for tasks like taking notes in meetings, grabbing coffee for the team, or addressing immediate, one-time needs. I should not maintain a long-term role that detracts from the responsibilities I need to be performing, not allowing others within the organization a chance to grow and gain experience or not to be held accountable.

Telling your leader what they shouldn't be doing might seem like the easiest form of leading up. That said, my initial response was defensive, leaning towards a "don't tell me what I can't do" attitude. After reflecting on her feedback, I realized she was right. I needed to either make a change, discuss options with my leadership, or delegate more effectively.

Another example from my career involves my tendency to think big and share grand ideas verbally with everyone. I enjoy brainstorming and strategizing with like-minded individuals and high performers. This involves discussing both immediate actions and long-term plans, even if they are uncertain. I often did this with various levels of employees within my teams.

One of my direct reports approached me with concerns about how this was negatively impacting the teams, explaining that my position and the way I presented ideas made it seem like we were committing to these big plans rather than just brainstorming. This left some staff feeling confused and perceiving constant shifts in direction. Initially, I dismissed her feedback, confident in my leadership and communication skills. I believed that if there were issues, they would have been raised directly with me.

However, she calmly pointed out that my energy, motivational style, and rank might prevent others who do not directly report to me from speaking up and saying they don't want to be involved in uncertain big-picture planning. She asked me to trust her judgment and consider her perspective. She suggested that we brainstorm together if that fulfilled my need for big-picture thinking. After reflection and a few more discussions, I understood and accepted her point. I adjusted my approach, limiting big-picture discussions to my inner circle, being very clear that this was a big-picture idea discussion when involving the broader team. This change led to clearer objectives and less stress for the entire department.

I can usually tell when my direct reports are leading up. While it might not be immediately apparent in the first meeting, as we all need time to process, I do try to wholeheartedly embrace their feedback through reflection, showing that I trust them for the positions I have placed them in, and that leadership is truly a two-way street.

As a follower, you can exert significant influence on your leader. You can change course, introduce new ideas, and alter the trajectory of many things simply by leading up.

As a leader, focus on learning when to scale back your leadership. Leading up involves difficult, open, and honest discussions about your priorities. A follower who comes to you and suggests scaling back on a grand vision has taken a major risk and shown real trust in your relationship.

Leaders often feel a passionate dedication to our ideas, believing them to be sound, productive, and headed in the right direction. As a leader, I rely on my followers to ground me when I'm confidently headed down a rabbit hole. Leaders are not infallible; we make mistakes. We're likely to make even more of them if we don't encourage our followers to lead up.

Throughout my career, I've encountered managers who were unaware of the realities of a situation or the likely impact of their plans. Leaders often focus on the bigger picture and expect their ideas to be quickly and precisely executed. However, this approach can sometimes overlook crucial details that determine the success of those grand ideas. This is where the concept of leading up becomes invaluable.

The Value of Leading Up

Followers leading up can help leaders recognize that speed and precision, when focused on the wrong target, will not help them realize their grand ideas in the long run. By providing honest and constructive feedback, direct reports can illuminate potential pitfalls and misalignments between a leader's vision and its practical implementation. They can highlight areas where the current direction might lead to inefficiencies or unintended consequences, allowing leaders to recalibrate their strategies before significant resources are expended.

For example, a leader might push for the rapid development of a new product without fully understanding the market needs or technical challenges involved. A perceptive team member, by leading up, can point out these oversights and suggest a more measured approach that ensures the product aligns with customer expectations and technical feasibility. This not only saves time and resources but also enhances the likelihood of the project's success.

In essence, followers leading up act as a critical check on the leader's ambitions, ensuring that the focus remains on achieving the grand vision effectively and sustainably. They help bridge the gap between strategic intent and operational reality, ensuring that the leader's ideas are not only grand but also grounded in practical wisdom. By embracing this dynamic, organizations can develop a culture where both leaders and followers contribute to the realization of shared goals, ensuring long-term success and innovation.

I once worked for an organization determined to venture into a new market with innovative products and services. The senior leaders and the Board of Directors were eager to swiftly bring this ambitious vision to life. The executive proposal, crafted by the vision's enthusiastic developer, was inherently biased and included unrealistic elements.

As a dedicated follower, I felt duty-bound to lead up by bringing these harsh realities to the attention of senior leadership. I scheduled several preparatory meetings with different leaders, meticulously documenting well-researched facts and figures. In each meeting, I emphasized that my recommendations did not mean we couldn't achieve their grand vision. Instead, I aimed to convince them that the required efforts, costs, and prerequisites necessitated a significant extension of the timeline.

During these meetings, I could see the excitement in their eyes dim slightly as I presented my findings. One senior leader, Mr. Thompson, furrowed his brows, his fingers tapping restlessly on the mahogany conference table. "Are you suggesting," he asked, "that our timeline is entirely unfeasible?"

"Not entirely unfeasible," I replied, choosing my words carefully. "But the timeline, as it stands, overlooks critical preparatory steps and underestimates the financial investment required. I believe a more extended timeline would ensure thorough execution and sustainable success."

Despite hearing me out, the leadership team decided to pursue their original plan. Faced with this decision, I resolved to lead up more challengingly than ever before. I approached my leaders again, my heart pounding in my chest. Respectfully, I noted that while I respected their decision, I found it difficult to support it without further discussion. "I believe a broader discussion involving all parties could help address these concerns comprehensively," I suggested.

My ability to influence the organization stemmed from the considerable time I had invested in connecting with my direct leader and cultivating relationships across all levels of leadership. When I started leading up, it felt like an uphill battle—eight against one. Everyone else believed a quick, easy, and cheap solution would suffice to achieve their goals. I repeatedly delivered unpleasant news about the projected outline, feeling like the harbinger of bad news at every turn.

In one particularly tense meeting, I laid out a detailed financial forecast, employee impact, and customer satisfaction concerns, showing the hidden costs and potential pitfalls. The room fell silent. I could feel the weight of their scrutiny, the skepticism hanging thick in the air. Finally, Mrs. Delgado, a seasoned leader, broke the silence. "You've certainly given us a lot to think about," she said, her voice tinged with concern.

Thankfully, the relationships I had cultivated paid off. Over time, the other leaders began to listen to me, leading to open, honest discussions and more realistic expectations. It was a difficult and frustrating process, filled with late nights and countless revisions of my presentations. But it was necessary. This example underscores why effective communication and relationship is a crucial component of leading up.

Had my efforts been in vain, I would have accepted the group's decision, albeit reluctantly. Yet, persistence and transparent communication paved the way for a more pragmatic approach. The leadership's final decision reflected a balanced understanding of the challenges and possibilities, a testament to the power of speaking up and the importance of patience in the face of resistance.

Anticipating Needs

Knowing your leadership well is crucial for effectively communicating with them. Building relationships is a great way to earn the equity you'll need to lead up. Building your relationships will provide you with insights on leading up more productively.

For instance, I know that my direct manager required a short but detailed analysis driven by black-and-white numbers. I provided a report well ahead of our one-on-one and group discussions. Other leaders needed different types of information to consider my concerns. One leader needed to understand the impact on employee engagement and relationships, another wanted to know about the impact on our customers, and another would want a combination of all areas (financial, employee, and customer impact) to start adopting my perspective. I met their needs by providing the necessary information before we met.

Anticipating your leaders' needs isn't limited to information. Based on our past interactions, I knew one leader would prefer to read a well-written document, another preferred verbal communication, and a third required a visual representation to grasp the bigger picture. Managing their preferences allowed me to earn short-term equity and ensure the leaders would be more receptive to the discussion.

You won't need to go to such lengths every time you need to lead up. You will need to choose your battles. Building relationships with your leaders will teach you about their preferences, enabling you to prepare and enhance your equity even when you're leading up.

In my case, the leaders were willing to listen because of the long-term equity I'd already built, and they focused on the issues I raised because of the short-term equity I earned by communicating in the most effective manner.

Anticipating needs is also an excellent way to build relationship equity even when you're not leading up. Anticipating their needs and getting ahead of small issues before they become major problems demonstrates your ability to think ahead, execute, and prevent negative impacts.

Effective Communication in Leading Up

Communicating information that people may not want to hear requires delicacy. Merely stating, "That won't work because..." is insufficient. You need to articulate your feedback in a manner your leadership is likely to consider.

For example, confronting an unprepared leader in front of a group will likely backfire. Effective discussions involve having preliminary conversations with your leaders to soften the blow and prepare them for the realities you need to share. As described above, this approach has served me well on numerous occasions.

Practical leading up gives your leader the chance to reconsider an unrealistic idea at their own pace, which saves face for them and creates a more effective path to averting a crisis.

Leading up is not a one-time discussion, especially when a group is involved. Groups tend to revert to the grand vision's unrealistic timetable. Followers engaged in leading up will have to steel themselves for difficult discussions and offer impeccable documentation to successfully steer the organization away from damaging directions.

Consider adopting a 'feedback-first' approach to effectively lead up without overstepping. Begin by asking permission to share your perspective, such as, "Would you be open to hearing some observations I've made about our current project direction?" This respectful opening will signal your intent to contribute constructively and prepares the leader to receive your feedback. Additionally, framing your suggestions as questions, e.g., "Have we considered the impact of X on our timeline?" can encourage collaborative problem-solving.

In most cases, followers should accept leadership's decisions and move forward supportively after your feedback has been considered, even if they don't agree. However, sometimes you must trust your instincts and push for more discussions, as I did.

Supporting your leader is essential; save these extreme measures for when they're absolutely necessary.

Building Relationships

Establish credibility with different levels of leadership in your organization. It is important to have a solid relationship with your direct leader, and expanding your network so that other leaders listen to you is equally crucial.

If you're a newer member of the organization, don't expect immediate trust or the ability to lead up. Invest in these relationships and demonstrate your abilities through your actions, not just words. Leaders must see you get results and witness your success, dedication, and practical communication skills regarding simple issues before they engage in any difficult conversations you want to have.

Cultivating relationships and managing your reputation allows you to have difficult discussions and lead up. Even when you try to lead up and fail, supporting the decision helps you maintain your influence. Building relationships is like making payments on a mortgage. Each interaction (or small payment) builds equity, and more significant contributions—like effective communication, achievements, support, and even difficult discussions—increase this equity. Having a good buffer of such organizational equity is crucial, as you never know when you may need to draw on it.

Professional equity and social capital with your leaders and peers refer to the value you accumulate in your professional relationships over time. This concept is similar to building social capital within your organization and involves cultivating a positive reputation, reliability, and mutual respect through consistent, constructive interactions. You establish personal equity by demonstrating competence, integrity, and collaborative skills in your dealings with superiors, colleagues, and direct reports. Building social capital is about the tasks you complete and how you handle them, communicate, and contribute to the team and organizational culture. Equity becomes a valuable asset, enhancing your influence, facilitating smoother collaboration, and leading to more significant opportunities for career advancement and personal growth within the workplace.

For example, if I hadn't built equity with my direct leader and other key decision-makers, I would have created more tension by pushing my leading-up limits. Instead, I leveraged my equity and other leaders' trust in me. I was able to achieve my objectives while maintaining positive relationships and my reputation within the organization.

Providing Solutions

I've been in many discussions where people highlight problems or the need for change but fail to offer solutions. Simply stating that there is an issue seldom works. A prominent feature distinguishing leading up from pointing out someone else's errors is that it involves coming up with solutions. Followers who come to me with issues and present even high-level hypothetical solutions receive more of my attention and time.

Sensitive issues may not always offer time to develop solutions. In such cases, being honest about urgency is crucial. This was starkly evident when a follower once approached me immediately after a pivotal meeting focused on a major organizational change. The atmosphere in the room had been tense, filled with a mix of anticipation and anxiety as we discussed the impending restructuring that would impact every department.

As the meeting adjourned, I noticed her lingering near the door, a troubled expression etched on her face. Summoning her courage, she approached me. "Do you have a moment to talk?" she asked, her voice barely masking the urgency behind her request.

"Of course," I replied, gesturing for her to sit down.

She took a deep breath before speaking, her eyes reflecting a mix of concern and determination. "I know we just concluded the meeting about the organizational change," she began, "and I understand the reasons behind it. However, there are serious concerns among the employees that I feel need immediate attention."

She explained that many employees were anxious about job security, fearing that the restructuring could lead to layoffs or significant changes in their roles without adequate preparation or support. Morale was already low due to previous changes, and the announcement had exacerbated these fears. "People are scared," she admitted. "There's a lot of uncertainty, and it's affecting productivity and mental well-being."

I could see the weight of responsibility she felt, even though she admitted she didn't have a proposed solution at the moment. "I might not be the right person to devise a solution," she confessed, "but I am willing to invest time in coordinating with the right teams to create one. We need to address these concerns before moving forward."

Her honesty was refreshing and underscored the immediacy of the situation. "Are you asking for a pause in the decision to have further discussions?" I asked, wanting to be sure I understood her request.

"Yes," she said, nodding emphatically. "I believe if we take a step back and engage with the employees directly, we can alleviate some of their fears and gather input that could lead to a more thoughtful and inclusive implementation plan. But we need to act fast. The longer we wait, the more trust we lose."

Her words resonated with me. The urgency was clear—this wasn't just about operational efficiency; it was about maintaining trust and morale within the organization. I knew that pausing the decision wouldn't be easy, but it was essential to ensure that the change was implemented smoothly and with the support of our employees.

"All right," I said, making a swift decision. "Let's schedule a series of discussions with the teams. We'll pause the decision temporarily to address these concerns. Your willingness to step up and coordinate this effort is exactly what we need right now."

Her relief was palpable. "Thank you," she said, a hint of a smile breaking through her worry. "I'll start organizing the meetings immediately."

This experience reinforced the importance of addressing sensitive issues head-on and the value of honest communication. It reminded me that sometimes, the most urgent matters require us to slow down and listen before forging ahead.

This is an excellent example of leading up. My follower approached me with her concerns, communicating them effectively despite her awareness of the urgency. Her prior investment in our collaborative work had built a substantial amount of credibility. She recognized my tendency to be visionary and presented straightforward data highlighting her concerns. She understood my preference for solutions and requested time to develop one. Ultimately, she leveraged her earned trust to suggest we have an additional discussion before moving forward.

Listening to her and acting on her concerns yielded significant positive outcomes. By pausing the decision and engaging in further discussions, we avoided several potential pitfalls. Firstly, we circumvented a significant drop in morale and productivity that could have resulted from unaddressed fears and uncertainties. Employees felt heard and valued, which promoted a sense of trust and collaboration across the organization.

Moreover, the input gathered during these discussions highlighted areas of the proposed restructuring that were previously overlooked. This allowed us to refine the plan, ensuring a smoother transition that was more aligned with the employees' needs and capabilities. As a result, we avoided costly missteps and resistance that could have derailed the initiative.

The positive results were evident. Employee engagement and satisfaction improved noticeably, as people felt more secure and involved in the process. The changes, implemented with greater care and consideration, led to enhanced efficiency and a stronger, more cohesive organizational culture. Ultimately, by taking the time to listen and adjust our approach, we not only preserved trust but also achieved a more successful and sustainable organizational change.

Conclusion

Above all, transparency is critical for leading up. Being transparent means being honest about intentions, open about concerns, and clear about objectives. Transparency acts as the binding agent in both personal equity and effective leadership. Engaging transparently means sharing information candidly and admitting to mistakes when you need to. Such behavior creates an environment of trust and respect, making it easier to influence and guide those above and around you.

Leading up is more than a skill; it is a mindset and a strategic approach that builds a culture of mutual respect and continuous improvement. By empowering followers to influence their leaders positively, organizations can harness a broader spectrum of insights and experiences, ultimately driving better decisions and more sustainable success.

To lead up effectively:

1. Cultivate Relationships: Building trust and social capital within your organization is the foundation of leading up. Invest in relationships with your leaders and peers, demonstrating your reliability and commitment through consistent actions.

2. Communicate with Purpose: Tailor your communication to meet the needs and preferences of your leaders. Use data, stories, and visual aids to present your ideas compellingly, ensuring that your message is clear and impactful.

3. Provide Solutions, Not Just Problems: When raising concerns, always come prepared with potential solutions. This proactive approach not only shows your commitment to the organization's success but also makes it easier for leaders to act on your feedback.

4. Anticipate Needs: Understand the priorities and pressures your leaders face. Anticipating their needs allows you to offer timely and relevant support, enhancing your credibility and influence.

5. Be Persistent and Patient: Leading up is not a one-time effort but an ongoing process. Be prepared for resistance and setbacks and maintain your commitment to constructive dialogue and improvement.

Reflect and Adapt: Throughout my career, I've learned that the most impactful leaders are those who remain open to feedback and are willing to adapt their approach. By embracing the practice of leading up and accepting when your followers are leading you, you contribute to a culture where everyone feels valued and heard, regardless of their position.

As you move forward, remember that leadership is a two-way street. Whether you are guiding others or being guided, your ability to lead up can significantly impact your organization's trajectory. Be bold in your efforts to provide honest, constructive feedback. Your courage to lead up not only enhances your leadership but also fortifies the entire organization.

In closing, consider this: Leadership is not about wielding power from the top down; it's about developing a collaborative environment where ideas and innovation flow freely in all directions. By mastering the art of leading up, you help create a more dynamic, resilient, and successful organization.

Take the First Step: Reflect on your current interactions with your leaders. Identify one area where you can apply the principles of leading up. Start small, build your equity, and gradually expand your influence. Remember, every step you take in leading up is a step towards a stronger, more effective organization.

Chapter 14: Listen Up & Read

Listen up! Got your attention?

Let's talk about something crucial: listening and reading. Whether you're a leader guiding your team or a follower absorbing information, these skills are fundamental. Don't just take my word for it—consider this: according to a study by Microsoft, the average human attention span has dropped from 12 seconds to just 8 seconds in the past decade (Microsoft Corp.). Meanwhile, a report from the National Assessment of Adult Literacy indicates that 43% of adults in the U.S. have low literacy skills (National Center for Education Statistics). This isn't just about reading words; it's about comprehending and retaining information.

Highlighting the Impact of Communication Skills

Recent studies by the Communication Institute for Online Scholarship highlight how practical listening and reading skills significantly impact team cohesion and decision-making processes. For instance, teams with members trained in active listening and critical reading techniques were 30% more effective in project completion and innovation metrics. These findings underscore the tangible benefits of refining our communication skills for personal development and the betterment of our organizations (Communication Institute for Online Scholarship, 2023).

We've all been in meetings where people are distracted, and we've all experienced projects where attendees haven't read the previous meeting minutes or meeting materials. What does this say about us? It highlights a significant issue: a widespread lack of attention to the written and spoken word. This can stem from being overwhelmed, not understanding our audience, or misaligning our organizational structures with our goals.

By addressing these challenges, we can enhance our communication skills, ensuring that both listening and reading become more effective parts of our daily interactions. So, let's dive into how we can improve these essential skills and, in turn, boost our overall productivity and understanding.

First, let's explore the barriers to effective listening and reading. In our fast-paced world, distractions are everywhere. From the constant ping of notifications on our devices to the pressures of multitasking, our attention is perpetually divided. According to Gloria Mark, a professor of informatics at the University of California, Irvine, it takes an average of 23 minutes and 15 seconds to refocus on a task after being interrupted. This constant interruption hampers our ability to listen and read attentively.

Moreover, the digital age has introduced a phenomenon known as "information overload." With vast amounts of information available at our fingertips, discerning valuable content from noise becomes increasingly challenging. Nicholas Carr, in his book "The Shallows," argues that the internet is changing our reading habits, making us more inclined to skim rather than read deeply. This superficial engagement with text diminishes our comprehension and retention abilities.

Improving our listening and reading skills starts with improving mindfulness. Being present in the moment and fully engaging with the material can significantly enhance our understanding. Here are some practical steps to get started:

1. **Eliminate Distractions:** Create a conducive environment for focused listening and reading. This might mean turning off notifications, finding a quiet space, or setting specific times for these activities.

2. **Active Listening Techniques:** Engage in active listening by paraphrasing what you've heard, asking clarifying questions, and providing feedback. This not only shows that you're paying attention but also helps reinforce the information in your memory.

3. **Deep Reading Practices:** Instead of skimming, allocate time for deep reading. Choose challenging texts that require you to think critically and reflect on the content. Take notes and summarize key points to enhance retention.

4. **Regular Practice:** Like any skill, listening and reading improve with practice. Dedicate time each day to read varied materials and practice active listening in conversations and meetings.

5. **Educational Tools:** Utilize tools and resources designed to improve literacy and listening skills. Online courses, audiobooks, and reading apps can provide structured learning experiences to enhance these abilities.

Improving these skills doesn't happen overnight, but with consistent effort, the benefits are substantial. Enhanced listening and reading skills lead to better communication, improved productivity, and a deeper understanding of the world around us. By prioritizing these skills, we can navigate the complexities of our information-rich environment more effectively.

So, as we journey through this chapter, let's commit to becoming better listeners and readers. By doing so, we not only improve ourselves but also enrich our interactions with others, creating a more attentive and informed community.

Being a top-level leader and follower requires immense involvement in reading and listening, particularly in engaging with the thoughts and ideas of those around you. As a leader, actively listening to your followers is crucial. It demonstrates respect for their perspectives, nurtures an environment of trust, and encourages open communication. When team members feel heard, they are more likely to be motivated, collaborative, and innovative. This kind of attentive listening helps leaders to identify issues early, understand the team's needs, and make more informed decisions.

In addition to listening, reading what your followers have written is equally important. Whether it's emails, reports, or informal notes, taking the time to read and consider their written communication shows that you value their input. It also provides deeper insights into their thoughts, ideas, and concerns, allowing you to respond more thoughtfully and effectively.

As a follower, listening to your leaders and reading what they have written is essential for alignment and effective execution of tasks. By attentively listening to your leaders, you gain a clearer understanding of their vision, goals, and expectations. This ensures that you are on the same page and can work more efficiently towards shared objectives.

Reading your leaders' written communication, whether it's strategic plans, memos, or casual updates, allows you to grasp the nuances of their directives and the context in which they operate. It helps you stay informed about important developments and better support their initiatives.

In essence, the interplay of listening and reading in both leadership and followership creates a foundation of mutual understanding and respect. This continuous engagement not only enhances communication but also builds stronger, more cohesive teams capable of achieving great success.

Listening

Listening goes beyond the mere act of hearing words. It's about fully engaging with the speaker and understanding their message. This is where the concept of active listening, or listening without interruption, comes into play.

Active Listening Defined - Active listening is the process of listening attentively while someone else speaks, paraphrasing and reflecting back what is said, and withholding judgment and advice. It's more than just not interrupting; it's about being fully present and engaged in the conversation. This means focusing on the speaker, observing their body language, and responding appropriately.

Key Elements of Active Listening

1. **Full Attention**: Give the speaker your undivided attention. This means putting away distractions and showing through your body language that you are engaged.

2. **Reflecting and Paraphrasing**: After the speaker finishes a point, paraphrase what they've said to show you understand. For example, "What I'm hearing is..." or "It sounds like you're saying..."

3. **Nonverbal Cues**: Nod occasionally, smile, and use other facial expressions to show that you are paying attention. Ensure that your posture is open and inviting.

4. **Avoiding Interruptions**: Resist the urge to interject with your thoughts or questions. If you do have a question, jot it down and wait for an appropriate pause or the end of the conversation to ask it.

5. **Responding Appropriately**: Once the speaker has finished, respond in a way that shows you have been listening. This could be asking a relevant question, providing thoughtful feedback, or summarizing what was said.

Why Active Listening Matters

If you take little else from this book, remember that listening is all about not interrupting. In the moment, it's almost too easy for us to interject with our thoughts, but if you cut someone off or start talking the second they stop, are you truly listening? People remember those who interrupt them—and not in a good way. It's human nature to be excited and want to share your ideas, but interrupting someone makes it seem like you think your thoughts are more important than theirs. If you interrupt someone, apologize and express that you are enthusiastic about the discussion. People are more likely to be understanding of those who admit to their shortcomings.

Sometimes, you might have a question when someone is speaking. If you're attending a presentation, ask if it's okay to interrupt for questions at the start. Use the raise hand option in video conferences. If someone is speaking in a meeting, and an intrusive idea or thought comes to mind, jot it down and then return to listening. Your notes need not be perfect; they are solely for you. Wait until the person has finished speaking, and then ask your question.

Engagement involves being present and listening with purpose.

The Power of "In the Moment Listening" & Eliminating Distractions

In an era dominated by virtual meetings, "In the Moment Listening" has become more crucial than ever. This means fully engaging with the speaker without letting your mind wander or multitasking. People can detect when you are not fully engaged with what they're saying, even if you respond appropriately. Multitasking undermines your relationships with others and makes it seem like you don't value what they have to say. Even if you think you're good at multitasking, you're not—and there's a wealth of research proving this. When you're having a conversation with someone, have the conversation. Your emails and other tasks can wait.

Nothing disengages a team or an employee more than divided attention, especially when it concerns your best and brightest. Listening in the moment will mean so much to those you engage with. If you listen, they will work harder and longer and be more loyal to you and your causes. A leader's job isn't to ensure tasks and operational functions are being completed; that's a manager's job. A leader's job is to listen and provide a space where your followers know that you are absorbing every word and genuinely trying to understand their perspective.

I've learned all this the hard way. I regret that I didn't understand the true importance of listening much earlier in my career! I heard people when they spoke and nodded along, but I wasn't listening. I was waiting to respond, crafting my response while they talked. My priority was being quick and dominating the conversation in favor of my agenda.

Eventually, I took a step back and reflected on my communication skills, and I realized the grave mistakes I was making by not truly listening. I am embarrassed of the disrespect I showed others, whether they recognized it or not, when I chose not to listen to them fully.

My natural communication skills are not geared toward listening, so I had to rewrite my learned behavior. Learning to listen was and continues to be an upward journey. Sometimes, I have to apologize after a meeting—distractions can still overtake my listening skills.

No one is perfect; you'll always have something on your mind or an urgent-seeming task list begging for your attention. Awareness is key to combating this. I have changed my learned behavior by cultivating awareness and preparing to listen to others as a top-of-mind practice.

Cultivating Awareness and Preparing to Listen

Awareness of Listening Habits

Cultivating awareness of your own listening habits is the first step. Here are some ways to become more conscious of your listening behaviors:

1. **Self-Reflection**: After conversations, take a moment to reflect on how well you listened. Did

you interrupt? Were you thinking about your response while the other person was speaking?

2. **Feedback**: Ask colleagues, friends, or family members for honest feedback about your listening skills. They can provide insights you might not be aware of.

3. **Mindfulness Practices**: Engage in mindfulness exercises to improve your focus and presence. Meditation can help train your mind to stay in the moment.

Preparing to Listen

To effectively prepare for listening, both mentally and physically, consider these strategies:

1. **Mental Preparation**: Before meetings, one-on-ones, and phone calls, take a few moments to clear your mind. Focus on the upcoming conversation and remind yourself of the importance of listening.

2. **Physical Environment**: Arrange your space to minimize distractions. If you're on a phone call, turn your chair away from your computer after answering the phone. Facing away helps you listen to the caller instead of continuing to work, reading emails, or being distracted.

3. **Video Calls**: For virtual meetings, ensure your workspace is free from distractions. Close unnecessary tabs and apps on your computer, and mute notifications. Remember, people can tell when your attention is divided.

4. **Technology Use**: Use tools that facilitate better listening. For instance, noise-canceling

headphones can help you focus during calls, and technologies, like AI, can transcribe conversations so you can review them later.

By cultivating awareness and preparing to listen, you can significantly enhance your communication skills and build stronger, more meaningful relationships. Remember, effective listening is not just about hearing words—it's about understanding and valuing the speaker's perspective.

Advanced Listening Skills & Navigating Complex Conversations: Advanced listening extends beyond merely hearing words; it involves empathetic engagement and reading between the lines. Techniques such as reflective listening, where you paraphrase or summarize what has been said to confirm understanding, create deeper connections. If you're dealing with conflict or a sensitive discussion, you must have the capacity to recognize emotional undercurrents and respond with empathy. Doing so aids in resolving issues and strengthens trust in professional relationships.

Reading: The Importance of Effective Reading Strategies

Like listening, effective reading strategies are crucial for professional growth. In today's information-rich environment, the ability to efficiently process and comprehend written material can significantly impact your professional development and success. Strong reading skills enable you to stay informed, make better decisions, and communicate more effectively.

Failing to cultivate these skills can lead to missed opportunities, misinterpretation of important information, and an overall lack of preparedness. For instance, not fully understanding a critical report or failing to grasp the nuances in a client's email can have negative consequences. Conversely, effective reading enhances your ability to absorb and apply information, adopting continuous learning and improvement.

Expanding on Effective Reading Strategies

1. **Skimming for Structure**: Before diving deep into any text, skimming for structure helps prioritize information and identify key points. Look for headings, subheadings, and highlighted terms to get an overview of the material. This initial scan provides a roadmap, making it easier to focus on the most critical sections during a more detailed read.

    - **Implementation**: When approaching a new document, spend a few minutes glancing through the headings, subheadings, bullet points, and any highlighted text. This quick survey will help you understand the document's structure and main topics. – But do not stop at skimming....read!

    - **Benefits**: Skimming allows you to identify sections that are most relevant to your needs, saving time and improving focus. It also prepares your mind to absorb and retain detailed information more effectively during a thorough read.

2. **The SQ3R Technique**: The SQ3R method—Survey, Question, Read, Recite, Review—is a proven strategy to transform passive reading into active engagement.
    1. **Survey**: Quickly glance through the text to get a sense of its structure and main ideas.
    2. **Question**: Formulate questions based on the headings and subheadings, which will guide your reading and keep you focused.
    3. **Read**: Read the text thoroughly, looking for answers to your questions.
    4. **Recite**: Summarize the key points in your own words to reinforce understanding.
    5. **Review**: Go over the material again to solidify your comprehension and retention.

- **Implementation**: Start by surveying the text to get an overview. As you read, write down questions that come to mind. After reading, summarize what you've learned and review the text to ensure understanding.
- **Benefits**: This method engages multiple cognitive processes, improving comprehension and memory retention. It transforms reading from a passive activity into an interactive one, making it easier to grasp and remember information.

3. **Recognizing Structure**: Identifying the structure of written communication—such as thesis statements, arguments, and conclusions—enables readers to critically assess and apply the information within their organizational context.

    - **Implementation**: While reading, pay attention to the introduction, which often contains the thesis statement. Look for topic sentences at the beginning of paragraphs that introduce arguments and notice how these are supported by evidence. The conclusion will summarize and restate the key points.
    - **Benefits**: Understanding the structure helps you follow the author's logic, making it easier to evaluate the validity of their arguments and apply the information effectively in your work.

4. **Active Reading**: Engage with the text by annotating, highlighting, and taking notes. This interaction helps to reinforce memory and makes it easier to locate important information later. Asking questions and making connections to existing knowledge can also deepen your understanding.

- **Implementation**: As you read, underline or highlight key phrases, write notes in the margins, and summarize sections in your own words. If something is unclear, jot down questions to revisit later.

- **Benefits**: Active reading transforms passive consumption into an active learning process. It aids in comprehension, retention, and recall, making the reading material more meaningful and easier to reference later.

5. **Regular Reading Practice**: Like any skill, reading improves with practice. Dedicate time each day to read a variety of materials—books, articles, reports, etc. This not only enhances your reading speed and comprehension but also broadens your knowledge base.

    - **Implementation**: Set aside specific times each day for reading. Vary your reading materials to include different genres and formats, such as fiction, non-fiction, news articles, and academic papers.

    - **Benefits**: Regular reading practice builds your reading stamina and improves your ability to understand and analyze complex texts. It also keeps you informed and intellectually engaged, which can enhance your professional capabilities.

Broadening the Scope

Effective listening and reading are vital across various professional settings. For instance, in healthcare, accurate patient care depends on precise communication, where miscommunication can have dire consequences. Medical professionals must read patient histories, medical literature, and treatment protocols attentively to ensure the best outcomes.

In the tech industry, understanding user feedback and reading market analyses are crucial for product development. Engineers and product managers rely on these insights to make informed decisions and drive innovation. Misinterpreting user needs or market trends can lead to costly mistakes and missed opportunities.

These examples illustrate that honing our listening and reading abilities is universally beneficial, whether in high-stakes environments or fast-paced innovative spaces. By developing these skills, we can improve our effectiveness, enhance our professional relationships, and achieve greater success in our careers.

Implementing Effective Reading Habits

1. **Create a Distraction-Free Environment**: Just as with listening, minimize distractions to improve focus. Find a quiet space, silence your phone, and close unrelated tabs or applications on your computer.

    - **Implementation**: Designate a specific reading area free from interruptions. Use apps or tools to block distracting websites and mute notifications on your devices.
    - **Benefits**: A distraction-free environment allows for deeper concentration and better comprehension of the reading material.

2. **Set Clear Goals**: Before you start reading, define what you want to achieve. Whether it's understanding a complex concept, gathering information for a project, or simply staying updated with industry trends, having a clear goal keeps you focused and motivated.

    - **Implementation**: Write down your reading goals and refer to them as you read. Break down large texts into manageable sections and set milestones for each reading session.

- **Benefits**: Clear goals provide direction and purpose, enhancing your engagement with the text and ensuring that you derive maximum benefit from your reading efforts.

3. **Take Breaks**: Avoid burnout by taking regular breaks, especially when reading dense or lengthy material. Short breaks help maintain concentration and improve overall retention.

- **Implementation**: Use the Pomodoro Technique—read for 25 minutes, then take a 5-minute break. Repeat this cycle and take a longer break after four sessions.

- **Benefits**: Regular breaks prevent mental fatigue, maintain high levels of concentration, and enhance your ability to retain and understand complex information.

4. **Discuss and Share**: Enhance your understanding by discussing what you've read with colleagues or peers. Sharing insights and perspectives can deepen your comprehension and provide new viewpoints.

- **Implementation**: Join a reading group or create one with colleagues. Schedule regular discussions to talk about what you've read and how it applies to your work.

- **Benefits**: Collaborative discussions foster a deeper understanding of the material, expose you to different interpretations, and enhance your critical thinking skills.

By adopting these strategies and cultivating strong reading habits, you can significantly enhance your ability to process and apply information effectively. Remember, effective reading is not just about absorbing content; it's about engaging with it thoughtfully and purposefully to drive professional growth and success.

In Conclusion

Effective communication lies in the words we speak as well as in the silence of our listening and the depth of our understanding. Active listening and diligent reading play a fundamental role in the realms of leadership and followership alike. Listening well challenges us to confront the distractions of our digital age and recommit ourselves to the art of being present—truly present—in every interaction.

In a world brimming with information yet starved for attention, listening and reading practices are the foundations upon which meaningful connections are built. Listening and reading bridge divides, enhanced collaboration, and drive our organizations forward with increased purpose. The active listening and reading strategies outlined in this chapter equip us to engage more deeply, think more critically, and lead more effectively.

I invite you to weave these skills into the fabric of your professional and personal life. To listen is to validate the voices around us, acknowledge their worth, and ask for the dialogue that drives innovation. To read is to open our minds to new perspectives, challenge our assumptions, and grow.

We can have a more mindful, engaged, and compassionate approach to communication—one that recognizes the power of our presence as the greatest gift we can offer to those we lead and those we follow. As you move forward, carry the lessons of this chapter as practices to live each day. In doing so, you may find that the key to unlocking your team's collective potential lies not in speaking louder but in listening closer and reading deeper.

Chapter 15: The Brilliant Non-Manager - Harnessing the Untapped Potential

Introduction: Recognizing the Unseen Pillars

In the grand theater of organizational success, leaders often enjoy the spotlight, but non-managers are the stagehands supporting every successful endeavor. This chapter explores the often-underestimated potential of the non-management workforce and strategies to harness their unique skills and perspectives for organizational growth. We will examine both the importance of leaders encouraging their brilliant independent contributors and the importance of those in more followership positions accepting that it is okay not to be a manager.

Non-managers, or individual contributors, are the specialists, the doers, and the creative thinkers who drive the core functions of the organization. Their direct interaction with products, services, and customers provides them with a unique vantage point, offering insights that can be pivotal in decision-making and strategy formulation.

Leaders must recognize when to allow non-managers—the followers in this case—to take the lead. In many organizations, leaders (managers, bosses, etc.) attempt to oversee every aspect of operations. While their intentions may be noble, this often hinders the organization's progress rather than aiding it.

Yes, the work may get done under such micromanagement, but at what cost? Are leaders inadvertently stunting their organization's growth by not allowing non-managers to take on greater responsibilities? The answer is unequivocally yes.

Leadership involves nurturing the growth and development of team members. If a non-manager displays brilliance in their work, the leader must encourage them, allowing them to shine and giving credit where it's due. This not only empowers the individual but also enhances the leader's reputation.

If a brilliant non-manager surpasses their leader, this growth reflects positively on the leader's ability to nurture talent and facilitate progression within the organization. Successful followers exemplify authentic leadership and the ability to recognize and foster excellence in others.

Effective leadership is not about asserting control over every aspect of operations but about empowering team members to reach their full potential. Leaders who embrace their followers' strengths and provide them with opportunities to excel can propel their organizations toward greater success.

Despite their critical role, non-managers are frequently underutilized, often confined to executing tasks without being encouraged to contribute to higher-level strategic discussions. This underutilization limits their potential growth and deprives organizations of diverse and innovative perspectives.

Personal Reflection: A Missed Opportunity

Early in my career, I witnessed a project led by upper management flounder despite dedication and hard work. Only later did I realize the missing piece was the insights and contributions of the non-managerial staff, who were intimately familiar with the ground realities but were never asked to contribute their perspectives. This was a pivotal moment in my understanding of organizational dynamics.

The Role and the Project: The project in question was the implementation of a new customer relationship management (CRM) system in our mid-sized company. I was an assistant project manager, working closely with the senior management team, which included the project lead—a highly experienced but somewhat disconnected senior manager.

The Consequences of Failure: The CRM system was critical for improving our customer service and sales tracking capabilities. Failure meant not only a significant financial loss—both from the sunk costs of the project and potential revenue from better customer management—but also a severe blow to the morale and trust within the team. The success of this project was expected to streamline our operations, reduce customer churn, and enhance our competitive edge in the market.

The Signs of Trouble: As the project progressed, it became clear that we were facing significant challenges. Despite our rigorous planning, the CRM system integration was plagued by technical glitches, resistance from end-users, and operational disruptions. The senior management team held frequent meetings to troubleshoot these issues, but our solutions were often temporary and superficial.

The Realization: One day, while discussing the project with a colleague from the customer service department, I was struck by the depth of their frustration. They pointed out several practical issues with the CRM system that had never surfaced in our management meetings. For instance, the system's interface was counterintuitive for the customer service reps, and certain features that were crucial for daily operations were either missing or poorly implemented.

This conversation made me realize that the non-managerial staff, who were the end-users of the CRM system, had not been consulted during the planning or implementation phases. Their hands-on experience with customer interactions and existing systems gave them valuable insights that could have preemptively addressed many of the issues we were encountering.

Changing Behavior: This realization was a turning point for me. I approached the senior manager and suggested that we hold a series of workshops involving the non-managerial staff, particularly those from customer service and sales. Despite initial resistance, my suggestion was eventually accepted out of sheer necessity.

During these workshops, the non-managerial staff provided crucial feedback that helped us identify and resolve many of the system's flaws. They suggested practical workarounds, highlighted critical features that needed adjustment, and even offered creative solutions to integrate the CRM more seamlessly into their workflows. Their input not only salvaged the project but also improved the final outcome beyond our initial expectations.

The Impact: The successful turnaround of the CRM project underscored the importance of involving non-managerial staff in decision-making processes. It became clear that their firsthand experience and ground-level insights were invaluable for realistic and effective project implementation.

As a result of this experience, I changed my approach to management and project planning. I began to actively seek input from non-managerial staff early in the planning stages of any project. I also advocated for a more inclusive culture within the organization, where everyone's voice could be heard and valued.

This shift in behavior not only improved the success rate of subsequent projects but also encouraged a more collaborative and motivated workplace. It was a lesson in humility and a powerful reminder that the brilliance of non-managers can often illuminate the path to success in ways that top-down management alone cannot achieve.

Strategies for Empowering Non-Managers

Empowering non-managers isn't just a nice-to-have; it's a strategic imperative that can transform an organization from within. When non-managerial staff are given the tools, opportunities, and recognition they deserve, they can drive innovation, enhance productivity, and contribute to a more dynamic and responsive company culture. Here are some key strategies to achieve this empowerment.

1. **Adopting a Culture of Inclusion**

   Create an environment where every voice is valued. It's essential to cultivate a workplace culture that actively seeks and respects the input of non-managerial staff. This means creating formal and informal channels for them to share their ideas, feedback, and concerns. Regular town hall meetings, anonymous suggestion boxes, and inclusive team discussions can ensure that non-managers feel heard and valued. When employees see their ideas being taken seriously and implemented, it boosts their engagement and commitment to the organization.

2. **Encouraging Cross-Level Collaboration**

   Promote collaboration between management and non-management staff to encourage more informed decision-making. Traditional hierarchical barriers often stifle communication and collaboration. To break these down, create opportunities for cross-level projects and initiatives. Joint task forces, cross-departmental teams, and mentorship programs can facilitate interactions between managers and non-managers. This not only leverages diverse perspectives but also helps build mutual respect and understanding across different levels of the organization.

3. **Providing Platforms for Contribution**

   Offer innovation hubs, suggestion programs, or regular brainstorming sessions where non-managers can share their ideas and insights. These platforms can take various forms, such as dedicated innovation labs, internal hackathons, or virtual idea boards. Encouraging non-managers to contribute their unique viewpoints not only brings fresh ideas to the table but also empowers them to take ownership of the company's success. Structured feedback loops ensure that ideas are reviewed and acknowledged, creating a continuous cycle of improvement and innovation.

4. **Recognizing and Utilizing Diverse Skill Sets**

Understand and leverage the diverse skills and experiences of non-managers to significantly enhance a project's success. It's crucial to identify the unique strengths of each team member and assign roles that align with their skills and passions. This can be achieved through regular skills assessments, one-on-one meetings, and personalized development plans. By recognizing and utilizing the diverse talents within the team, managers can ensure that everyone is working to their fullest potential, leading to more effective and innovative project outcomes.

5. **Training and Development Opportunities**

Invest in the professional development of non-managerial staff to boost their morale and enrich the organization with a more versatile workforce. Offering continuous learning opportunities, such as workshops, online courses, and certification programs, helps non-managers develop new skills and advance their careers. Additionally, creating clear pathways for career progression within the organization can motivate employees to strive for excellence. By prioritizing their growth, companies not only enhance their internal capabilities but also build a loyal and motivated workforce.

Implementing these strategies requires commitment and effort, but the rewards are substantial. Empowered non-managers contribute to a vibrant, innovative, and agile organization capable of navigating the complexities of today's business landscape. By fostering a culture of inclusion, promoting cross-level collaboration, providing platforms for contribution, recognizing diverse skill sets, and investing in training and development, companies can unlock the full potential of their non-managerial staff and drive sustained success.

Expanding on Training and Development

In any organization, investing in the continuous growth and development of employees is crucial. Training and development programs not only enhance the skills and competencies of the workforce but also foster a culture of learning and improvement. By providing structured development opportunities, companies can nurture talent, increase job satisfaction, and ensure long-term success. Here, we explore two key strategies for empowering non-managers: mentorship programs and leadership development tracks.

Mentorship Programs

Mentorship programs are a powerful tool for professional growth, facilitating the transfer of knowledge, skills, and experience from seasoned professionals to emerging talent. A well-structured mentorship program can significantly impact employee morale, engagement, and retention.

DeltaCorp, a leading technology firm, recognized the need to bridge the knowledge gap between its experienced leaders and its non-managerial staff. By implementing a mentorship program, the company aimed to create a supportive environment where non-managers could learn from the expertise of their mentors. Mentors provided guidance on career development, technical skills, and industry insights, while mentees brought fresh perspectives and innovative ideas to the table.

DeltaCorp's mentorship program pairs non-managers with leaders in their field, fostering an exchange of knowledge and skills. This initiative has led to a marked increase in employee satisfaction and retention, illustrating the value of investing in non-managerial talent as a cornerstone of organizational growth.

The program's success was evident in several key metrics. Employee satisfaction surveys showed a significant increase in positive feedback, with participants highlighting the value of personalized guidance and support. Additionally, retention rates improved as employees felt more connected to the organization and saw clear pathways for their career growth. DeltaCorp's experience underscores the importance of mentorship as a strategic investment in talent development.

Leadership Development Tracks for Non-Managers

Leadership development tracks are designed to identify and nurture high-potential non-managers, preparing them for future leadership roles. These programs provide structured training, hands-on experience, and opportunities to demonstrate leadership capabilities.

EcoWorld's Leadership Development Track: EcoWorld, an environmental NGO, established a leadership track for high-potential non-managers, offering workshops, shadowing opportunities, and project leadership roles. This program has prepared a new generation of leaders and reinforced a culture of internal growth and opportunity.

EcoWorld, dedicated to environmental conservation and advocacy, needed strong leaders to drive its mission forward. To ensure a steady pipeline of capable leaders, the organization created a leadership development track specifically for non-managers. This track included a series of workshops on leadership skills, opportunities to shadow senior leaders, and roles in leading key projects.

The impact of this program was profound. Non-managers who participated in the leadership track reported increased confidence and readiness to take on leadership responsibilities. By promoting from within, EcoWorld reinforced a culture of internal growth, demonstrating to all employees that dedication and potential would be recognized and rewarded. The program also fostered loyalty and commitment, as employees saw clear opportunities for advancement within the organization.

Why These Quotations Matter

The quotations from DeltaCorp and EcoWorld highlight the transformative potential of targeted development programs. They emphasize the critical role that mentorship and structured leadership tracks play in cultivating non-managerial talent. These initiatives are not just about improving individual skills; they are about building a robust, adaptable, and committed workforce that can drive organizational success.

In the broader context of organizational growth, these examples illustrate how investing in non-managerial staff can lead to significant, measurable benefits. Employee satisfaction and retention are directly linked to the opportunities for growth and development provided by the organization. By learning from these case studies, other companies can adopt similar strategies to unlock the potential within their own non-managerial workforce, ensuring a more dynamic and resilient organizational structure.

Training and development programs like mentorship and leadership tracks are essential components of a successful organizational strategy. They help build a pipeline of skilled and motivated employees who are prepared to lead and innovate. By prioritizing the growth of non-managers, companies can create a more inclusive and empowering workplace, ultimately driving long-term success and sustainability.

Call to Action

Harnessing the untapped potential of non-managers requires leaders to recognize the wealth of talent within their ranks and then take deliberate steps to engage these individuals. This process includes conducting organizational audits to identify gaps, establishing task forces focused on implementing empowerment strategies, and committing to regular progress reviews. Organizations that follow through on these actions can ensure that non-managers' brilliance is recognized and integrated into their path to success.

When acknowledged, non-managers' brilliance can lead to remarkable organizational achievements. Many of the most innovative, successful strategies emerge from their insights. Therefore, leveraging the potential of the non-management workforce is critical for any organization aspiring to thrive.

The path to organizational success is not solely in the hands of those at the helm but in the equally capable hands of the non-managers. These unsung heroes, with their direct line of sight to the operational realities, customer experiences, and innovative solutions, drive progress. When nurtured, their potential can transform the projects they work on and the organization itself. In this chapter, we've explored strategies to bridge the gap between leadership aspirations and ground-level insights, advancing a culture of inclusion, collaboration, and empowerment that transcends traditional hierarchies.

The examples from various sectors and the actionable strategies offer a blueprint for leaders willing to look beyond conventional wisdom. They underscore the importance of creating platforms for contribution, recognizing diverse skill sets, and investing in development opportunities that elevate the entire workforce.

As leaders, we must stop viewing non-managers as mere followers and recognize them as the co-creators of our organizational success. Let's commit to dismantling barriers, encouraging cross-level collaboration, and building a culture where every voice is heard. It's time for leaders to embrace this untapped potential, acknowledging that the future of their organizations lies in the hands of those who commit their skills and passion to the collective mission.

Leaders can unlock a reservoir of potential that propels their organizations to new heights. The journey toward leveraging your organization's full spectrum of talent begins with a simple shift in perspective that recognizes every individual contributor's inherent capability.

Let this chapter serve as a call to action: to elevate, empower, and celebrate the non-managers whose brilliance is the cornerstone of true organizational excellence. In doing so, we pave the way for a more comprehensive and dynamic workplace and chart a course toward unprecedented success.

Chapter 16: The Road Ahead: Continuous Growth in Leadership, Followership, and in Life

As we draw this book to a close, I hope you've come to see that the journey of leadership, followership, and achieving work-life harmony does not end here. I want this book to be the spark that ignites our imagination and supports intentional development.

Our professional and personal lives are filled with unforeseen challenges and growth opportunities. This final chapter is a gateway to continuous development and fulfillment.

Embracing Change

Change is the only constant, at work and in our daily lives. Embracing change, therefore, becomes a pivotal skill for any leader or follower. Adapting, learning from new situations, and remaining flexible will set you apart in the long run. We are made to endure; adapting to change provides opportunities to cultivate that endurance.

The Imperative of Lifelong Learning

Lifelong learning guides us toward sustained growth and relevance. Leadership and followership mean continuously updating your knowledge base, refining your skills, and expanding your perspectives. Pursuing new understanding and capabilities is essential, whether through formal education, self-study, or observed learning. Continuous learning enriches your professional life and enhances your personal development, ensuring you remain an asset to your team, organization, and family.

Consider thinking outside the box when it comes to learning. In navigating the intricate balance of professional and personal life, cultivate a mindset of diversity in obtaining knowledge. Embrace innovative and unconventional approaches to education, recognizing that wisdom flows not solely from the senior's experience to the junior's eagerness but often in reverse. The fresh perspectives and insights of junior members can enrich the knowledge base of more experienced counterparts.

A reciprocal exchange of wisdom nurtures an environment of continuous growth, where everyone is valued and heard regardless of their position or tenure. Remember that the most profound lessons often arise from the most unexpected sources.

Developing Resilience and Well-being

Cultivating resilience—your ability to bounce back from setbacks—is key to recovering from challenges along life's path. Attending to your mental and physical well-being will bolster your resilience. Mindfulness, regular physical activity, and engaging in hobbies and activities that rejuvenate your spirit will help. Self-care practices serve as the foundation upon which your resilience is built, enabling you to navigate the complexities of your professional and personal life.

Work-life balance and self-care cannot be confined to a one-size-fits-all solution. They are deeply personal and uniquely tailored to what brings joy and fulfillment to everyone. If a particular activity or practice brings you happiness without causing harm to yourself or others, embrace it fully. Craft a version of self-care that inspires and motivates you. Let your self-care reflect your inner needs and desires, not a performance for outside admiration.

Adopting Meaningful Connections

The relationships you develop are invaluable. Connections provide support, offer new insights, and enrich your life in countless ways. Prioritizing these relationships—nurturing them with attention, empathy, and respect—creates a network of mutual support and shared growth. Leadership and followership are not just about directing or following; they are about connecting with others, understanding their needs, and working together toward common goals.

Leading with Purpose and Integrity

As you move forward, let purpose and integrity be your guideposts. Knowing why you do what you do, aligning your actions with your values, and maintaining ethical standards are the hallmarks of true professionalism. Living your values inspires trust, raises loyalty, and creates an environment where everyone is encouraged to bring their best selves to the table.

At its core, leadership, and followership embody the essence of partnership—a dynamic collaboration built on mutual understanding and a shared belief in progressing together. Love unconditionally, step up to lead when the moment calls for it, and have the humility to follow when that is your role.

Without partnership, we are wandering in circles. Actual progress stems from this symbiotic relationship, where leading and following are not fixed roles but fluid responsibilities shared for the greater good. In this partnership, we find our direction, purpose, and collective strength to move forward.

Finally

The road ahead, with its unique challenges and rewards, is yours. The principles of effective leadership, proactive followership, and work-life balance outlined in this book are tools to aid you on your journey. Your commitment to growth, learning, and balance will ultimately define your path.

As you close this book and look to the future, remember that leadership and followership are a mosaic of continuous learning, resilience, and meaningful connections. Move throughout your journey with curiosity, compassion, and an unwavering commitment to personal and professional development.

The road ahead is rich with potential—embrace it with an open heart and a willing spirit, ready to shape a fulfilling career and a life of balance and joy.

Whether coming or going, leading or following, never underestimate your potential.

The End & Thank you for investing your time in reading!

I would also like to take a moment and thank the many people in my life who encouraged me to take on this endeavor. Your motivation, positive feedback, constructive feedback, and unwavering support have meant more to me than I will ever be able to express.

If you enjoyed this and would like to stay connected and review additional works similar to this book, please consider connecting with me. See below of additional information.

Website: www.weareleadership.com

Or use the QR code below for my website:

LinkedIn: https://www.linkedin.com/in/mikecomptonleadme/

Use the QR code below for my LinkedIn profile:

Newsletter - I also produce a regular newsletter on leadership, followership, and general development topics via LinkedIn.

Use the QR code below to access my newsletter:

Podcast: Listen to my podcast, "Leading the Way by Mike Compton," available on Spotify, Amazon Music, Apple Podcasts, and iHeartRadio.

Use the QR code below to access my podcast on Amazon:

Made in United States
Troutdale, OR
03/12/2025